The Didsbury Lectures, 1990

CHRIST AND CREATION

The Didsbury Lectures

The Didsbury Lectures are delivered annually at the
British Isles Nazarene College, Manchester

Previous series are available as follows:

* These titles available from Eerdmans

CHRIST AND CREATION

Colin E. Gunton

THE PATERNOSTER PRESS
CARLISLE

WILLIAM B. EERDMANS PUBLISHING COMPANY
GRAND RAPIDS, MICHIGAN

First published jointly 1992 by The Paternoster Press,
P.O. Box 300, Carlisle, Cumbria, CA3 0QS, UK,
and Wm. B. Eerdmans Publishing Co.,
255 Jefferson Ave. SE, Grand Rapids, Michigan 49503.

Printed in the United States of America

British Library Cataloguing in Publication Data

Gunton, Colin E.
Christ and Creation
I. Title
232
Paternoster ISBN 0-85364-527-2

Eerdmans ISBN 0-8028-0579-5

Typeset by Photoprint, Torquay, Devon

Contents

To Christoph and Marlene

Preface

I was greatly honoured by the invitation of the Nazarene Theological College to deliver the 1990 Didsbury lectures. To the honour of the invitation was added the generous welcome and hospitality of the Principal, staff and students during the time I spent with them. Here, now, is the outcome: four lectures, only slightly revised for publication, following the advice to that effect of members of the College and of my own colleagues. Major revision would have involved the consideration of a number of topics excluded for reasons of space, and so changed the nature of the work which, as it stands, is a summary dogmatic christology, a proposal, which will, I hope, provide opportunities for further thought, whether in agreement or otherwise.

In revising the lectures I have taken into account some of the many pertinent points made by members of the attentive and generous audience. I am also grateful to colleagues and students at King's College, especially, as always, Dr Christoph Schwoebel. Professor Graham Stanton and Dr Francis Watson were particularly helpful in commenting on my use of biblical material, while members of the King's College Research Institute in Systematic Theology heard and discussed drafts of the lectures and helped to improve them.

Colin Gunton
King's College, London
March, 1992

An Interpretation of Scripture

I Approach to Interpretation

In 1983, I wrote a study of christology whose most perceptive critical reviews came privately in the form of letters. Wrote Professor T. F. Torrance: 'you can follow this up by a study of the closer relation of Incarnation to creation, which will strengthen your case.' And from Dr Geoffrey Nuttall came the remark that 'in a rounded christology the Holy Spirit should have more than four references.' And so the agenda for this series of lectures was set. For, as I hope to show, those two criticisms are complementary, almost two sides of the same coin, and it is in the doctrine of the Holy Spirit that are to be found many of the clues to a more adequate study of Christ and creation.

So much for the general theme of the lectures. In this first, I shall attempt 'an interpretation of scripture,' and for one reason in particular. I believe that all faithful Christian theology must be in some way or other an interpretation of the scriptures of the Old and New Testaments. There are reasons for this belief, some of which will emerge in the course of the lectures. But at this stage there is need for one in particular to be stated: that it is in scripture that Christ and creation are first related. In this first lecture, accordingly, there will be attempted a brief outline of some of the main things there said or suggested: some generalisations about what seems to be scripture's teaching about Christ and creation. These generalisations will be made in fear and trembling, for a number of reasons, but in the expectation that there is more to be found that is relevant to our topic than is commonly believed.[1] The reason for the expectation is *theological*: that we miss things that are to be found in the pages of the Bible because we are not accustomed, for various reasons, to look for them. Certain things have been missed because the tradition of interpretation has not led us to expect them. What they are will appear below, as, in later lectures, will the names of some of the theologians who have encouraged a wider quest.

But before that, the question of modern interpretation must at least be raised. In the modern age one may speak neither as though modern historical criticism had not happened nor—and this is the weakness of those who give too much weight to critical interpretation—by evading the contribution of a whole tradition of interpretation from the first days of Christian theology. All interpretation is shaped by the frameworks of belief which we bring to it; the hope is that the text—or rather the Holy Spirit's opening up of the text—will enable us both to use and to transcend those frameworks with ever new insights into the truth of the gospel. In what, with decreasing confidence in recent days, we call the modern era, it has often been claimed

---

1. One of the reasons for anxiety is, of course, the way in which demarcations between the theological disciplines make it a fearful thing to tread upon others' ground. I am therefore particularly grateful to my colleagues Graham Stanton, who read drafts of the first two lectures and made some helpful suggestions; and Francis Watson, whose sharing in the life of the King's College Research Institute in Systematic Theology has much enriched its life, and who also made some valuable suggestions.

that dispassionate study of the scriptures reveals that there is no such thing as *the* teaching of Scripture on any given topic. There is no overall unity, because the Bible is more like a cave full of scrolls than a unified work of theology.[2] Although it must be conceded that there is something to justify the metaphor, we are also justified, with the help of an ever increasing bibliography, to question the critical orthodoxy that appeared, until even quite recently, to have carried all before it, and at the same time to question also the dogma of total diversity. What is to be attempted is a looking at the scriptures with eyes that have been trained in the critical disciplines and yet beyond them in a hope of discerning something of a general unity in the writings.

It is, without doubt, the unity that is the problem. Here it should be freely acknowledged that past generations have sometimes attempted to impose too rigid a unity on the canon. The problems may be said to have begun with the attempt of Origen and some of his predecessors to argue that in some way every text of the Bible can be understood to have an inspired significance. (The result of this is that the written text somehow *replaces* the living Spirit). Similarly, attempts in the aftermath of the Reformation to develop concepts of inspiration often provided the wrong defences against growing critical attacks, depriving the biblical authors of their humanity and in the process making it more difficult than it should have been for nineteenth century England to come to terms with Darwinism and other scientific theories.

The metaphor of the cave full of scrolls reminds us that one achievement of the critical movement is, to

---

2. There is an interesting discussion of this question in Gabriel Josipovici, *The Book of God*, New Haven and London: Yale University Press, 1988.

teach us that there is no monolithic unity to scripture. The writers were human beings whose particularities and weaknesses—among other things—marked all that they had to say. Yet that is not to say that, as happened with the most rationalistic of the critics, we may treat them as ignorant primitives, prescientific mythologizers only dimly aware of the world in which they lived. One of the things that we may gladly learn from some of the more recent work of the biblical specialists is the individuality and sophistication of the theologies of the different writers. To this we may add that they belonged, and knew that they belonged, to a great literary tradition.

The unity of the Bible, however, is not in the end a literary or historical–critical question, but a theological one. To discern within the pages of the Bible in all its diversity, problems and richness the being and action of a single God is a matter of faith. It is not in the last resort something we can discover for ourselves. If it were, there would be rather less disagreement than there is about the reality and status of holy writ. Faith, however, is not the same as blind faith. For theology, faith does two things at least. It orients us to the place where God is to be found; and it drives us to seek understanding. That is the lesson that Karl Barth learned from Anselm of Canterbury, and it is noteworthy, although often missed, that it can be seen to apply to other areas of thought and culture than the simply theological. Michael Polanyi, classically, has argued, appealing to Augustine's 'If you do not believe you will not understand', that, despite widespread claims to the opposite effect, such is the underlying rationale of modern science.[3]

If the faith that finds witness to a single God in

---

3. Michael Polanyi, *Personal Knowledge*, London: Routledge and Kegan Paul, 1958, pp. 266f.

Scripture is a faith that seeks understanding, the first uncomfortable phenomenon with which it must come to terms is the variety in the ways that the Bible's God is understood to come into relation with the world he has made and redeemed. A Christian systematic theology must find its unity and coherence within that variety and diversity, not by denying it. And that is where we must combine with modern critical studies an inter-action with the wisdom of the past. The theological tradition, in its wisdom, has discerned a number of themes running through the books of the Bible. In that sense, it has not itself been monolithic, for it has often noticed that some themes are more stressed in some places than others, while others have to be looked for if they are not to be missed. The key to a modern theological interpretation of scripture will be to take account of the richness and variety, without losing sight, or better, in order to gain some vision of, the one God to whom Scripture bears witness throughout its pages.

One example of a theme that has in the past assumed great dogmatic importance, sometimes on the strength of what appears to be rather minimal evidence, is the ascension of Jesus. I introduce it here because it is of some importance for the theme of the lectures, and will concern us in particular in the final lecture. On the face of things, the ascension is treated in rather few places in the New Testament, and then rather var-iously. Yet if the writings are approached with eyes seeking out allusions and theological developments, it will come to be seen that the theme is far more pervasive than appears.[4] Similarly, J. G. Gibbs has argued for the pervasiveness of the theme of Christ the

---

4. See William Milligan, *The Ascension and Heavenly Priesthood of Our Lord*, London: Macmillan, 1901, chapter 1. I am much indebted to Douglas Farrow for an introduction to the importance of this topic.

Creator in the New Testament.[5] So also, I shall argue, is it with other dimensions of our theme which are not so often recognised.

The chief methodological point, however, is that the unity of scripture is to be discovered in large part in terms of a (limited) number of ways in which it represents the relations between God, the human race and the world. It would take a full systematic theology to attempt to bring the various major themes into relation to each other, and the best systematic theologies have done this without forcing the text too narrowly into a straitjacket. What is being attempted in this first lecture is an approach to scripture's various ways of representing the relation of Christ and creation, with questions in mind which have been suggested by the adequacies and inadequacies of the tradition. Is it possible to discern something like a unified teaching? May we speak, without imposing a premature or false unity on the text, of Christ and creation? What dimensions of the topic are suggested by scripture? It will then be the task of later lectures to test these beginnings dogmatically. There the chief question will be of whether they enable us to articulate a coherent vision of the world, so that the worship and life of the church may be fed, so that conversation may take place with modern culture and so that life in the world may be illuminated and enriched.

II Lord

Who, then, is the Christ of the Bible, and what is his relation to creation? That is the first question. And, given the modern suspicion of appealing directly to

---

5. J. G. Gibbs, *Creation and Redemption. A Study in Pauline Theology*, Leiden: Brill, 1971.

dogmatic formulations like those that form the usual quarry for this topic, let us begin with the gospel portrayals of Jesus. In these, one does not have to read far to find that Jesus is portrayed as one who bears the authority of the Lord of creation. 'Who then is this, that even wind and sea obey him?' (Mark 4:41). Matthew's variant on the saying is interesting, for reasons that will become apparent: 'What sort of man is this, that even winds and sea obey him?' (8:27). If there is something in common to the Synoptic portrayals of the relation of Christ and creation, it is first of all to be found here. Jesus in some way or other is or represents the Kingdom of God, so that what he does is concerned, again in some way or other, to establish or re-establish the promised reign of God on earth. That reign includes not only what we sometimes mistakenly call the 'spiritual' and moral realm, but also the material. It includes healing as well as teaching, the driving out of the demons that bring parts of the creation into slavery, and the miraculous multiplication of loaves and fish. A similar authority over creation is depicted in the Fourth Gospel, for example in the miracle at Cana, even though in such cases the writer is chiefly concerned with the symbolic representation of christological claims.

Here, however, we must pause to look at the miracles. It has been customary in some modern interpretation to distinguish between those miracles with which the modern can come to terms—for example, by claiming healings to be psycho-somatic or the feeding of the five thousand to be really a 'miracle of sharing'—and those, particularly 'nature miracles', which appear to have no 'point' to them. If we are to understand the meaning of the miracles as they are presented to us, we must put on one side all those attempts, particularly by nineteenth century rationalistic interpretation, with its mechanistic view of the universe, to explain away what is presented to us. Not only are such artifices now made obsolete by changes in cosmology, but they obscure the point that the reign of God realised in the ministry, death and resurrection of Jesus does not distinguish as we sometimes do between spirit and matter. Creation is one, and its redemption does not make that kind of distinction. In that sense, all of the Synoptic miracles, and in a different way John's carefully chosen selection, are signs and instances of the reign of God taking place on earth. There is room for argument about how far the gospel writers may be supposed to intend to present Christ lord of creation, but it seems to me at least implicit in what is presented. And it can be added that the use of imagery from nature in many of the parables points to the place of the order of creation in the gospel view of the Kingdom. The general point is that the stilling of the storm shares with the healing of demoniacs the characteristic of being an aspect of the redeeming action of the one endowed with divine authority over all the world. The language used in the stilling of the storm—'be silent'—is the same as that used in some of the accounts of exorcism. We have here and in many other places a militant reestablishment of the rule of God over a creation in thrall to evil.[6] The actions are representations of the authority of Christ over creation.

In the background of that redeeming action of Jesus is a range of Old Testament phenomena and teaching. First is the fact that in what he does in and with the created order, Jesus is anticipated by a number of Old Testament figures, particularly the prophets, who are also presented as healing and raising the dead. The authority of Jesus over creation reveals, to use the language particularly of the Reformation tradition, both his kingly and his prophetic offices, his continuity with

---

6. I owe to Francis Watson this point and that about the parables.

the Old Testament 'anointed'. Aware of this, we shall acquiesce neither in attempts, both ancient and modern, to use the miracles as proofs of the divinity of Jesus, nor in rationalistic attempts to explain them all away. Establishing the divinity of Christ is not a matter of abstract proofs but of discerning in what happens, from birth to death, resurrection and ascension the action of the incarnate Word. Yet in the free authority revealed in all the accounts, we are enabled to find one greater than the prophets. Jesus' lordship over the creation reveals his perfecting, his being the culmination, of patterns of divine-human action begun in those who come before him.

The second relevant feature of the Old Testament background is the conception of creation to be found there. According to this, creation is one, all of it deriving from the word of the creator. It is not therefore to be interpreted dualistically in terms of two orders, such as matter and mind, as happened in most Greek thought. Further, equally important and an implication of the foregoing, humankind is depicted in close symbiosis with the rest of the world. Genesis chapter 3 makes it quite clear that moral and physical ills are interdependent, so that redemption from them will likewise involve a healing together of what we call moral and what we call physical. Similarly, the Fall involves a loss of that dominion over creation which is one dimension of the human calling. Despite the ecological problems caused by human misuse of the created order, we should not be afraid to appropriate the notion of dominion. More direct treatment of the topic must await a later lecture, but it is possible, and, I believe right, to interpret the kingly and prophetic work of Christ, in teaching and miracle alike, in terms of a re-establishing and perfecting of the dominion given to the first human creatures. That is the gospels' version of the Adam–Christ typology of Paul. Here is true Adam

exercising the dominion that hitherto the human race
had failed to achieve. The healing of the demonically
afflicted, the most potent signs of the bondage of the
created order to decay, also makes sense on this
interpretation.

There is a further feature of the Old Testament
account of creation which is of immense importance for
our theme, for it, like the second, concerns the relation
between creation and redemption. I have claimed that
Jesus, when he heals and performs miracles, is establishing the promised rule of God over all things. A
recent paper has argued that from the beginning there
is in any case a close relation between creation and the
ordering of human life within it. From his examination
not only of the Old Testament but of other ancient
creation literature, H. H. Schmid concluded that in
many ancient cultures a conception of creation serves as
a framework for cosmic, political and social order.
Conceptions of salvation—of true human life on earth
and in society—are framed within beliefs about the
creation of the world. Hebrew thought is no exception,
and Schmid argues that 'the belief that God has created
and is sustaining the order of the world in all its
complexities, is not a peripheral theme of biblical
theology but is plainly the fundamental theme. What
Israel experienced in her history and what the early
Christian community experienced in relation to Jesus is
understood and interpreted in terms of this one basic
theme.'[7] If that is so, the framing of Jesus' ministry by
conceptions of his relation to the whole of creation is
not incidental to it, but an essential dimension.

In the gospel accounts of his ministry, then, Jesus
is depicted in different ways as being lord of the

---

7. H. H. Schmid, 'Creation, Righteousness and Salvation: "Creation Theology" as the Broad Horizon of Biblical Theology,' *Creation in
the Old Testament*, edited by B. W. Anderson, London: SPCK, 1979,
pp. 102–117 (p. 111).

creation. By his words and actions he re-establishes the rule of God over it, bringing in the promised eschatological kingdom. We have seen that some of his acts are anticipated in the works attributed to the prophets. Yet what we have here suggests something beyond what they achieved. There is a freedom, uniqueness, consistency and universality that appears to place him in a different category from his forerunners. Here we have something greater than those representative Old Testament figures, Jonah and Solomon (Mt. 12:41f). What we are to make of this will be the subject of the rest of the lectures. Here, we are on the threshold of the central christological question: in what sense is all this the work of a man, in what sense of God, the lord of creation?

III God

Long before the gospel accounts of Christ's lordship of the creation came to take their present form, even more radical theologies of his relation to the creation had become part of the earliest Christian confessions. J. G. Gibbs has argued in connection with one of the first of the passages, I Corinthians 8:6, that in view of the way it is introduced, as a quotation of something it appears to assume the reader will accept, it is likely to be the citing of an early Christian credal confession.[8] The interpretation is not uncontroversial. J. D. G. Dunn inclines to accept neither that interpretation nor even the claim that it makes Christ a co-agent in creation. His interpretation of the parallel ascriptions of creation to God the Father and the Lord Jesus Christ is more minimal: 'Christ, who because he is now Lord shares in God's rule over the creation and believers, and therefore his Lordship is the continuation and fullest

---

8. Gibbs, *Creation and Redemption*, p. 59.

expression of God's own creative power.'[9] Dunn's interpretation is not very convincing, particularly in view of what the words actually say, and appears to be determined by his evolutionary view of the development of christology. The view is far more convincing that under the impact of the resurrection the belief developed early that one whose relation to God was of such a kind was, indeed, the one through whom God made the world. The remark Moule makes in connection with his interpretation of the christology of Colossians appears better to fit the case. 'It is worth the effort to recall that these stupendous words apply . . . to one who, only some thirty years before (and possibly less), had been crucified.'[10] However remarkable the claim, whatever the origin of the words used to express it, and however incredible may appear the content, there appears to have developed soon after the death of Jesus a widespread Christian confession to the effect that the one through whom God had acted to save the world was also the agent of its creation.

The 'cosmic christologies' of the New Testament have received much treatment over the years, and there is little point in doing more than summarise what the most convincing interpreters say of them. The first point is that in general they associate Christ with God the Father in creation, while at the same time distinguishing them from one another. The distinction may be made by means of a preposition, so that creation is *from* God the Father and *through* Christ (I Cor 8:6), or it may be done as the Fourth Gospel does it, by attesting the universality of the Word's agency in creation: 'without him was not anything made that was

---

9. James D. G. Dunn, *Christology in the Making. An Enquiry into the Origins of the Doctrine of the Incarnation*, London: SCM Press, 1980, p. 182. The passage is there printed in italics.

10. C. F. D. Moule, *The Epistles of Paul the Apostle to the Colossians and to Philemon*, Cambridge University Press, 1962, p. 58.

Feb. 1:2

made.' For the Letter to the Hebrews, similarly, the Son is the one 'through whom . . . he created the world.' There is enough in those passages alone—and they are not alone—to give credence to Gibbs' contention that the mediatorship of creation by Christ belongs to an early and widespread Christian credal belief.

Worthy of note also is the tensing of the verbs used of Christ's part in creation. Many of them, perhaps, and in John's case almost certainly, echoing the first chapter of the Bible, attribute to Christ creation 'in the beginning.' We have already heard the words of John and Hebrews in this tense, and could add Colossians' 'in him all things were created' (1:16), noting, however, the not easily construed preposition. To the past tense is often added, sometimes in the same passage, a present tense. The one through and in whom all was created is also the one through whom they are upheld in the here and now. Hebrews is a case in point, with its 'upholding the universe by his word of power' (v. 3). And then there is the future tense, used eschatologically of the directedness of all things to Christ. The Fourth Gospel, consistent with its relative, though not total, lack of interest in a future eschatology, does not stress this aspect, which is found for the most part in later writings in the Pauline corpus. In Colossians, there is a teleological but not strongly eschatological note: 'that in everything he might be preeminent' (1:18). Ephesians strengthens this reference, by placing the mission of Christ in eschatological perspective: 'a plan for the fulness of time, to unite all things in him, things in heaven and things on earth' (1:10).

Col. 1:16

The effect of the introduction of present and future tenses is to link creation with redemption. It is to reinforce the point taken from Schmid that doctrines of creation are central to the outworking of other doctrines. The theologies of the cosmic Christ are not pieces of independent speculation but are designed to bring out the meaning of Christ for the completion of that which was in the beginning. One important early passage is 1 Corinthians 15, where the implications of the resurrection for the present and future reign of Christ are spelled out. Here, as in the gospels, little effort is made to distinguish the human from the divine Christ. It is to the man Jesus that significance appears to be attached. Yet parts of the chapter clearly give to the risen Christ the significance of deity, and particularly a prominent share in the reign of God. That share is, in the first place, a present reality, as verses 25 and 27 imply. But the reign is not immediate or timeless: it is teleological, directed to an end, and the end is the conquest of all the foes of God, ultimately of death. (It is significant that death is also among the enemies to be defeated according to the eschatology of Revelation, see for example 20:14). If we are to do justice to the cosmic and sheerly material contents of Paul's chapter, we must not spiritualize away the meaning of death in this passage. Death as we now experience it is something that reigns in the created order as the result of its fallenness. The death of death that is instituted by the resurrection does not mean the end of dying, but the promise that death will be swallowed up in life. Only God, the one who is both creator and redeemer, is able to achieve the redemption of the cosmos signalled by the resurrection. Christ, the agent of that redemption, is therefore inseparable from God the Father in the completion of creation that is called redemption.

When passages such as those which have been discussed are added to the passages in which the preexistence and eschatological future of the Christ are introduced without direct reference to his relation to the creation, it seems clear that we have here more than a few proof texts culled arbitrarily to prove a dogmatic point. The facts that they come strategically at the beginning of treatises like those of John and Hebrews, that they appear to be used unselfconsciously as part of the fabric of early Christian belief, and that they are not inconsistent with—to understate the matter—the lordship over creation depicted in Synoptic narratives, are pointers to something of considerable significance. Whatever we may wish to make of them—and of the Old Testament and other background—in 'the modern age', and I want to make much of them, there can be little doubt that, for whatever reason, they bulked large in early Christian response to the resurrection of Jesus from the dead. It may be our weakness, not that of the New Testament, that so little has been made of these passages constructively in recent christology.

IV Man

In the synoptic portrayals of Christ as the Lord of creation, we find the ground both of the explicit doctrines of Christ the creator to be found in the epistles and of the patristic doctrine of the incarnation. The latter will be treated in a later lecture. But we now reach a matter of which less has traditionally been made, but which is essential to any adequate treatment of Christ and creation. They are the places where we see quite clearly that Christ is not only lord of creation, but also part of it. An interesting point here is that ascriptions of humanity to Christ, or passages implying it, often appear within the very passages we have been exploring as pointers to Christ the creator. According to Colossians 1:18, for example, Jesus is the first-born from the dead, an attribution putting him alongside other created beings, as well as over them. Similarly, the so-called kenotic christology in Philippians 2 appears to lay side by side on the one hand a narrative of divine action, rooted in eternity but happening in time, and on the other a pattern of human behaviour and death corresponding to it. There is correspondence between the divine and human dimensions of the meaning of Christ, as we have already seen in connection with the reign of Christ as it is expressed in I Corinthians 15.

It is, of course, for the most part taken as read in the New Testament that Jesus is a full human being. The Letter to the Hebrews makes one of the few explicit affirmations in saying that Christ was as we are in all things, sin apart. The qualification is an important one, for it implies something about what it is to be a creature. Sin is not part of what it is to be human, but a distortion of our humanity. In being like us in all things, sin apart, Jesus is depicted as authentically creaturely, the human creation in its integrity. (That is why his lordship over the creation has the freedom and authority that is quite different from that of the other servants of God). But it is not a bloodless humanity: he weeps, is angry, deliberately offensive, even, apparently, on one occasion violent. What appears to be the key to his humanity is the integrity at once of his life's direction and of his relation to one he calls his Father.

There are five themes in the New Testament where, it may be suggested, there are narrated or recorded events crucial for our apprehension of the unique humanity of Jesus. The two most clearly linked are the temptation and the accounts of his dying. The temptation stories locate the truth of his humanity in his response to the Father: 'You shall worship the Lord your God, and him only . . .' (Luke 4:8). The accounts of the crucifixion likewise tell something of the saving significance of the human suffering as it is undergone in relation to God. I believe that the words of dereliction as recorded in Mark and Matthew much used, even overused, as they are in recent theology, should not be understood chiefly as something happening between the Son and the Father, between God and God, as Moltmann has famously suggested, but as telling us something about the human relation of the *incarnate Son to God the Father*. It is as a representative human being that Jesus shares the experience of Godforsakenness, just as it was as a representative Jew that he freely accepted the baptism of John. The one without sin is thus made sin: placed in the relation to God that is theirs who by their sin put themselves under judgement. It is thus the climax of the human story of the one who accepted baptism for the remission of sins and shared the temptations of humankind. There will be more to say of this in the next lecture.

The third theme brings us to an area of greater ③ controversy. There has been much argument recently over the necessity or otherwise to Christian belief of the doctrine of the virgin birth of Jesus. A recent contribution is that of C. E. B. Cranfield who has argued for the uniqueness and authenticity of the accounts of the virgin birth of Jesus over against those who would dismiss them by assimilating them to patterns of contemporary religious thought.[11] Here, once again, as with other miracles, we must set on one side a long tradition of attempting to use the virgin birth as a kind of proof of the divinity of Jesus. If we read carefully, I believe, it will become apparent that the accounts have more to do with the reality and character of the human Jesus: of his being as part of the created order. Karl Barth has famously linked together Virgin Birth and Resurrection as miracles at the beginning and end of Jesus' earthly life, and the dogmatic justification of such a claim will be examined later. But it is doubtful if those few writers who refer directly to it—it is, of course, a matter of some controversy whether John, for example, in some way alludes to the teaching—are concerned primarily with miracle in the modern evidential sense.

---

11. C. E. B. Cranfield, 'Some Reflections on the Subject of the Virgin Birth,' *Scottish Journal of Theology* 41 (1988), pp. 177–89.

They are rather concerned with its place in the divine redemption of the world: it is these human beings, mother and child, whom God uses as the basis of a new act of creation. It is here significant that the only genealogy given in connection with his birth, Matthew's, traces Jesus' human lineage to Abraham, the father of the faithful.

 The fourth central dimension of the New Testament theology of the humanity of Jesus is the resurrection. Again, we must be cautious of those attempts which have been made to prove the divinity of Jesus through the resurrection. There may be something in them; at the very least, the resurrection demonstrates a divine verdict on the ministry and death of Jesus. Pannenberg, for example, has made much of the fact that the resurrection in the midst of time—rather than at its end—of one man—rather than the whole of humankind—can be made the basis of an argument for the more than merely human significance of Jesus. But it is important to remember that the resurrection has much to do with his human significance. The speeches in early chapters of the Acts of the Apostles, addressed as they are to chiefly Jewish audiences, concentrate on bringing out Jesus' messianic significance. The resurrection is the positive verdict of God on the one condemned to death by his own people.

There are three general points that are made either by the New Testament writers or on the basis of what they say which bring out the significance of the resurrection for our understanding of Christ the creature. The first is that it *makes universal* the significance of Jesus of Nazareth. That this man among all the nations of the earth is chosen for the anticipation of the end at once reveals and makes real his significance for the whole of reality. In illustration it is enough to refer to the fact that the resurrection was the basis of the mission that led out into the world a faith that possibly even in Jesus' eyes was limited to the Jewish people; or, if a less Pauline example is required, the belief in the universal rule of Jesus over the nations in the book of Revelation.

The second point is that the resurrection justifies the ascription to Jesus of a certain *exemplary* significance. Not only is he the first born of all creation, but he is the first among many. One way in which the Bible expresses the relation between Christ and humankind concretely is by its use of Adam/Christ typology. The typology is justified by the resurrection, but is traced back to the very beginning of Jesus' ministry. In contrast with Matthew's, Luke's genealogy, by appearing at the beginning of the ministry and tracing the line back to Adam 'the son of God' (3:38), makes links with another dimension of the biblical treatment of Jesus' humanity, the relation with Adam. As always, christology and soteriology are in close relation. As Adam represents fallen humanity, so Jesus is true man in the image of God, and demonstrated to be so by virtue of his resurrection. The theme is one Paul made his own, but can be seen to be quite consistent with Lucan accounts of the temptation. The temptations of Jesus are adamic at least in the sense that they show a refusal of disobedience which contrasts with the story of Adam. Similarly, the teaching that Christ is the image of God links up with what was argued to be the message of the gospels about Jesus' lordship of creation. 'Col. 1:15 is also concerned with the events of creation. Christ is not only eikon tou theou, as was Adam, but also king over creation in a way vastly different from the first man.'[12] We can on this basis say that Irenaeus' theology of recapitulation, that Jesus is

---

12. Robin Scroggs, *The Last Adam. A Study in Pauline Anthropology*, Oxford: Blackwell, 1966, p. 97.

the one who relives the human story in direct inversion
of the adamic pattern, has plentiful basis in scripture.

The third point is that it appears to be clear that for
the New Testament the logic of the resurrection was
eschatological, in that it implied a return of Christ to, so
to speak, complete the story. This point has been
brought out by Robert Jenson,[13] and appears to have
more to be said for it than Pannenberg's theory of the
'retroactive' significance of the resurrection.[14] (The
resurrection is 'retroactive' in one sense, in that it
realises the significance of Jesus even for those who
lived before him, but not, I would argue, in terms of his
relation to God, as Pannenberg would have it). Resurrection, rather, implies, a return in glory. Whether or
not it is true that the earliest Christians expected, and
were then disappointed in, a rapid return of Jesus—and
the evidence, despite generations of assertion of the
claim, continues to be lacking—the logic appears to be
constant. The one who rose will return, to judge the
quick and the dead. Are they not still praying for a
return of the Lord in glory in the time of the
Apocalypse?

The eschatological dimensions of the resurrection
bring out other features of the relation of Christ and
creation. In the first place, it relates Christ directly to
the creation. As the giving of life out of death it
demonstrates the power of God over the created order,
and becomes the basis of the doctrine of creation out of
nothing, as the words of Romans 4:17 make clear: 'who
gives life to the dead and calls into existence the things
that do not exist.' It clearly, also, carries meaning which
is, as Pannenberg has claimed, inherent within it when

---

13. Robert W. Jenson, *The Knowledge of Things Hoped For. The Sense of
Theological Discourse*, London: Oxford University Press, 1969.
14. Wolfhart Pannenberg, *Jesus—God and Man* translated by L. L.
Wilkins and D. A. Priebe, London: SCM Press, 1968, pp. 135–141.

it is understood in its context.[15] Much has been made of the differences of the accounts of the resurrection appearances, particularly between those of Paul and of the gospels. Yet there is something they have in common, and that is a note of transformation within continuity. The risen Jesus is not an immaterial spirit, but one with a body eschatologically transformed. Flesh and blood, indeed, do not inherit the kingdom (1 Cor. 15:50), and yet it is *this* body which is transformed: the perishable puts on imperishability.

As the one to whom is given the life of the age to come, the transformed Jesus becomes also the source of that life for others. Here the significance of Jesus becomes more than simply exemplary and we can no longer separate what he does as man, what as God. Not only is he acknowledged as the one true human being, but also, by virtue of his resurrection, the source to others of the same quality of life that he had himself exercised. Paul here contrasts Adam with Christ, quoting Genesis: ' "The first man Adam became a living being"; the last Adam became a life-giving spirit' (1 Cor. 15:45). It is here that talk of the resurrection's saving significance shades into a discussion of our fifth theme, the ascension. In the Fourth Gospel, whose chief interest is in the incarnation, the ascension is the completion of what happened in the passion, the completion of the process of Jesus' return 'glorified', to the Father, and a condition for the coming of the Spirit.[16] Only after the ascension is Jesus the one who mediates the Spirit. For the Letter to the Hebrews, the ascension is central in a slightly different way, and enables us to round off this brief rehearsal of some of the biblical accounts of the relation of Christ and

15. Pannenberg, *Jesus*, pp. 74–88.
16. C. K. Barrett, *The Gospel According to St John*, London: SPCK, 1962, p. 470.

creation. As the Fourth Gospel looks back at the incarnation from the point of view of life in the Spirit, for this writer all is said in the light of the ascension. Jesus is the priest who by virtue of his faithfulness and obedience offers to the Father the true sacrifice that is a perfect human life. As the one who has returned to the Father he becomes the eternal source of salvation to those who believe but *as one who is still on the side of the creation.* 'For because he himself has suffered and been tempted, he is able to help those who are tempted.' (Heb 2:18, noting the present tense, and cf 5:2). He is as man the eternal bridge between heaven and earth. We shall have far more to say about the significance of the ascension in future lectures. But the allusion to it does raise one final question which is of central interest for a modern discussion of Christ and creation.

V Cosmic Saviour?

How far may it be said that the whole creation, and not merely the human race, is to be saved through Christ's work? How far, for example, does Christ's sacrifice of himself imply also the perfection of that world from which his flesh was taken? Today, with all our ecological guilt and anxiety, we are perhaps over-concerned to play down the anthropological dimensions of the gospel and to stress the broader context of the whole of creation. The topic must be approached with caution, particularly in view of the fact that reactions to an acknowledged ill often take the form of over-reactions. Thus today there is much talk of creation-centred spirituality, sometimes as if it were the creation and not the creator that we worship. In many places there is to be found a tendency to pantheism, the pagan and dehumanizing effects of which will reveal themselves all too soon. If they are to be avoided, it must be remembered that it is not creation that was made in the image of God, but man and woman.

In this area, an element of anthropocentrism is inevitable and good. This is not because we are so to elevate the human race above all the rest of creation that we may do what we wish with it, but because if there is an ecological problem it is we who are the centre and cause. The universe could no doubt go its own way without us. Similarly, if the Word becomes flesh, it is because the involvement of God with the world in the man Jesus is the means by which the created order is reconstituted in its relation to God. What is to be avoided is not all anthropocentrism, but the tearing apart of creation and redemption, so that redemption comes to appear to consist in salvation out of and apart from the rest of the world.

The relation of creation and redemption will be a continuing theme of future lectures. Our concern here, however, is with how far the New Testament promises a redemption of all things, not merely the human race. It has to be said that there is very little suggestion that the created world is of interest apart from us, its most problematic inhabitants. The whole creation may groan in travail, and indeed, awaits its redemption from futility, but it is the redemption of the children of God that is at the centre, even in Romans 8. The new heaven and new earth of the Apocalypse is, again, largely, the stage on which the slaughtered and risen lamb will rule the nations. Perhaps the nearest we come to a promise of redemption for the whole universe is in Ephesians 1, where there is room for dispute about what is meant about the reconciliation of 'all things'.

What cannot be denied is the point already made with the help of Schmid's paper, that there is in the Bible no redemption, no social and personal life, apart from the creation. It is therefore reasonable, especially in the light of Old Testament witness to the creation, to hold that the Bible as a whole is concerned with the future of creation, particularly in view of the evidence we have reviewed from the Synoptic Gospels of Christ as Lord of creation. But the fact that it is Israel and Jesus who are at the centre of God's action in and towards the world means that it is the personal that is central, the non-personal peripheral. That does not rule out an ecological concern, but it cannot be of independent interest. The creation is represented before God first by Christ and then, in dependence upon him, by us.

VI Conclusion

In this first lecture, I have sought to present in summary salient aspects of the New Testament teaching about Christ and creation. There are to be found passages which teach unequivocally that Christ is lord of creation, and lord in such a way that he must be understood to be the one through whom it was made, in whom it coheres and to whom it moves. Equally important, there is clear teaching that Christ is part of creation like us, or at least as we are created to be. He is not the saviour apart from his humanity. There have been some references to dogmatic or systematic concerns, but the question has not really been raised of how we are to take this teaching, that is, whether the twofold claim is true or even coherent, and how far the church has been right to develop its christology in the way it has. In future lectures, I shall hope to isolate and discuss the main systematic questions which arise.

Christ the Creature

In the first lecture, an attempt was made to summarise the salient ways in which the New Testament, against the background of the Old, expressed the relationships between Christ and creation. I suggested that one neglected dimension of these relationships was that in which Jesus is depicted as being part of the creation, and it is the dogmatic possibilities of this dimension that I wish to explore today. It may, indeed, appear that dogmatic is the word, in a bad as well as theologically respectable sense, for I shall of necessity be rather summary. But if an outline of so momentous a topic is to be essayed in four lectures, that is how it must be. The point to be made here is that what I am offering is a proposal: of a way to conceive the relations of Christ and creation, without making any attempt to justify every stage of the argument.

None the less, this is not to be open and criterion-less speculation. The question at the centre is whether the development of the themes makes possible an illuminating conversation between the Bible, ourselves and the world in which we live, with the different partners in the conversation throwing light upon each other. The chief criterion accordingly will be whether faith attains a greater measure of understanding of what it is to be a human creature before God and in the world. I shall therefore begin with a speculative theology of what, in general, it is to be a creature, and particularly a human creature, before moving on to ask the question of the respects in which Jesus is, as a creature, the same as and different from the rest of the human race. Each enquiry, that concerning ourselves and that concerning Jesus, will fall into two parts.

I Aspects of the 'Horizontal'

To be a creature is to be constituted, to be made what one is, by and in a network of relationships. For want of better words, and provisionally only, we can say that these relationships are, ontologically, twofold: vertical and horizontal. I am using the terms as a metaphorical way of indicating relations with, respectively, God and the rest of creation. Let us examine the latter first. To be a creature is to be constituted by, and to constitute, other finite beings existing in space and time. This is not, of course, what could be called an absolute constituting, out of nothing. All 'horizontal' constituting depends upon the fact that there is, both temporally and logically, prior to it, a constituting of the world by God. That is the concern of the next section. Here, my concern is with the relationality that is made real, at the finite level, by the fact that there is a creation of which theology speaks: that God has made a world of such a kind that there is within it the mutual constitutiveness of which I wish to speak. An illustration of this matter is provided by the fact that one or two people have recently asked me whether faith in God would be under threat if scientists were to be able to 'create life.' The fact is that they would not be so able. They may be able to constitute life in the sense of being able in laboratory conditions to replicate the conditions in which life takes shape, but that is not a proper way of speaking of creation, for they would simply be using materials already to hand. It is in that sense that I am using the concept of constitution in this section of the lecture.

There are various ways in which this basic fact about the universe can be illustrated. One example of the horizontal networking of all things is given in relativity theory and its recent development, that everything in the universe is related to, in part dependent upon, everything else for what it is. But there is given in this not an undifferentiated network of relations. The universe is not a blank homogeneity. Rather, there is a network of mutually constituting *particularities*: distinct beings who yet take the shape of their being from one another. To take a simple illustration, we can say that a relatively small and short-lived creature like an insect is constituted for brief span of time out of the reservoir of being by certain causes—procreative, sustaining and the rest—and returns to that reservoir once its brief cycle of life is complete, possibly after sharing in the constitution of others of its own species. To identify all the constitutive causes of even so minor a link in the great chain of finite being is a task of daunting complexity, where investigation requires a degree of abstraction from the many possibilities open to the enquirer. But the general point is clear enough, as is an additional one that the particularities with which we are concerned are what they are in terms of their relatedness in what we call time and space. They are bounded before and behind, above and below, and this boundedness, which is by no means uniform in character—there, apparently, being different 'times' and 'spaces'—is an ineradicable qualification of their being; is, in fact, what we mean by 'time' and 'space'.

It is a far more difficult matter to account for the horizontal constitution of more complex and long-lived organisms, and especially of human beings. To account for the constitution of the person, we abstract a number of diverse agencies and influences, corresponding to the overlapping sciences in which the human race is studied. Some of these are what we would call impersonal. Thus for a human being to come into existence and survive there is continuing dependence upon the material world. Human dependence upon food and water has always been understood in general, but to such basic common sense have been added over the centuries increasingly complicated scientific analyses, chief among them the biological. Few would now deny some form of evolutionary contribution to the development of the shape that human life now takes, or that much of what we are derives from the structure of our genes and from what we eat.

Only biological reductionists, however, would affirm that such is the whole story. We are also what we are by virtue of what our histories and our social context make of us. To be English in the late twentieth century is to be in certain ways, of course difficult to specify, different from what it is to be French or Mongolian. I do not want to suggest that all the English or the Chinese, or who you will, share a common way of thinking or uniform way of living, but that where and when we are has something to do with who we are: with our particular being, or *hypostasis*. Even more crucial for our particular constitution are those responsible for our birth, upbringing and education—those, that is, most closely bound up with us in our particular network of relations. That I was educated in a school with a tradition of pushing pupils in the direction of the ancient universities will have had certain incalculable effects on the kind of thought that is emerging into light of day in this lecture. And so one could go on.

Our constitution is a kind of determination, a making determinate in time and space. In many of the determinants of our lives, we have no choice: of genes, parents, sex, nationhood and the rest. What there is of freedom will have something to do with what we see ourselves as making of our determinateness. The important fact to hold in mind is that we are what we are, horizontally speaking, by virtue of these relationships and what we make of them. It is part of the complexity of this matter that there is a wide range of ways of understanding the balance between self- and other-determination of our being. A sociological determinist, for example, will want to explain all of what we are by our social past and present, while different accounts of our psycho-physical determination will be given by Freudians and disciples of B. F. Skinner. We live in a world offering not only a variety of scientific and ideological accounts of who and what we are, but of rival and incompatible ones too. I believe that few of the various and often competing accounts can be rejected outright, but also that few of them are free of ideological and theological or anti-theological content. The very untidiness of the picture should encourage us in the belief that theology may have something to contribute to the conversation of the disciplines, although whether it can do it in the form of the kind of unification that Pannenberg has suggested in his study of theological anthropology must be open to question.[1]

One major complexifying factor in all this is the additional theme that our relationships with the world and with each other have a personal and moral dimension. By this I mean, to put it in a simple and metaphorical way, that the different ways in which we shape and experience our combination of determination and freedom make for life, or they make for death. We make or break ourselves and each other by the way we

---

1. Wolfhart Pannenberg, *Anthropology in Theological Perspective*, translated by M. J. O'Connell, Edinburgh: T & T Clark, 1985.

live together in the world. The horizontal aspects of what has traditionally been described as sin encompass the way in which personal relationships are disordered, and so are in different ways destructive rather than constructive of humanity. We know that hatred brings about a diminishment of both hater and hated, while the pumping into the atmosphere of large quantities of smoke damages human relations with the world about us, as well as disrupting the balance of nature. Increasingly we are realising, with the help of modern physics, that everything is related to everything else, so that all human actions, as well as all that happens in the non-personal world, affect in different ways everything else that there is. It is in this context strange that Sallie McFague claims the opposite to be the case: 'in our time . . . there is scepticism concerning the unity of all that is.'[2] This is odd at a time when relativity physics is telling us precisely that the universe is an interconnected system of relativities. Her argument will hold only by the kind of separation of the human and historical from the cosmic that is becoming increasingly untenable in a world in which the disciplines are drawing together, not further apart. It also depends upon a systematic confusion between relativity and relativism, the distinction between which is of extreme importance. If the fluttering of a butterfly's wings over Peking can affect next month's storms over New York, it would appear to be a fortiori true that human culture and activity should be related to other parts of the world in a way that makes it relative to them. But that is not the same as *relativism*, which, at least in its radical forms, is a doctrine that denies the kind of objective truth claims made in that statement, because it holds

---

2. Sallie McFague, *Metaphorical Theology. Models of God in Religious Language*, London: SCM Press, 1987, p. 6.

that beliefs are merely relative to the persons or cultures that hold them.

When we say of Jesus that he is of one substance with ourselves, sin apart, part of what we mean is that, like us, he was a particular human being, a determinate person, made what he was in part by his genes and the history and society of the world in which he came to be. Therefore no christology is adequate which tries either to evade the material determinateness of Jesus or his Jewish particularity. Here we must reject out of hand any idealizing of Jesus, such as that which is sometimes found in modern theology, which in any way minimizes the importance of his Jewishness. It is part of the blessing and scandal of particularity that the Jews were and are the elect nation, and that Jesus came from their midst. We can therefore agree with John Robinson when he writes of the need to take seriously the particular genetic inheritance of Jesus.[3]

What we must not do, however, is to take this so far as to suggest that evolutionary or any other science is able to give a full account of his significance, any more than it can explain the whole of our determinate particularity. Corresponding to the Scylla of an idealizing of Jesus—the liberal protestant, catholic liberationist or bourgeois feminist face reflected from the bottom of the deep well—there is the Charybdis of scientific determinism. Here, it is essential to be aware of the increasing recognition of the partial nature of the sciences. It is still easy in our culture to treat the sciences as the vehicles of omniscient explanation of all that is. To the contrary, recent discussion of the history and philosophy of science has made it clear that the sciences abstract, taking from the whole a part in order to understand one of its determinants, but in so doing

---

3. J. A. T. Robinson, *The Human Face of God*, London: SCM Press, 1973, p. 42.

disqualifying themselves from understanding the whole. This would always have been understood had it been recalled that all human knowledge is finite, because the human capacity for understanding is limited.[4] It follows, then, that we cannot understand, on the basis of our genetic inheritance alone, the ways in which we are what we are, because they are equally effected by the way our families have loved—or failed to love—us, and our churches have or have not embodied the gospel.

When we turn to consider Jesus' particular humanity in its 'horizontal' relationships, we are limited in a number of ways in what we are able to say of his historical and religious constitution. Although the evangelists are more interested in his biography, broadly understood, than some modern scholarship has suggested,[5] they are theological biographers— evangelists!—with an axe to grind. Thus certain episodes, like Luke's account of the boy Jesus' encounter with the teachers in the temple, have been abstracted by the evangelists from the tradition to make particular theological points. On a different level, critical scholars are able to draw parallels between the reported teaching of Jesus and that of the Wisdom and apocalyptic traditions, showing or suggesting his determinate place in the history and religion of first century Judaism. One of the immense debts we owe to recent scholarship is for its presentation to us of Jesus the Jew. But unless we

---

4. See, among the many recent discussions, John Ziman, *Reliable Knowledge. An Exploration of the Grounds for Belief in Science*, Cambridge University Press, 1978 and Richard Boyd, 'Metaphor and Theory Change. What is "Metaphor" A Metaphor For?', in *Metaphor and Thought*, edited by A. Ortony, Cambridge University Press, 1979, pp. 356–408. 'Physical laws are abstract idealisations of regularities which are rarely exactly mirrored in the real physical world . . . . In general, physics deals with artificially closed systems . . .', Keith Ward, 'Acts of God', unpublished paper.
5. Graham N. Stanton, *Jesus of Nazareth in New Testament Preaching*, Cambridge University Press, 1974.

are historical or sociological determinists, we shall not accept that as a complete or final account of his humanity. The very paucity of the evidence suggests that the evangelists and others were at least as interested in what he made of his Jewish inheritance as in its determination of his being and activity.

What we are presented with in the gospels is chiefly that set of relationships in which the writers saw the particular significance of Jesus to consist. What made for life and for death—his death—in Jesus' case was the network of relationships he had with particular groups of people and with the material world. The crucial relationships chosen for presentation in the gospels can, for the most part, be seen as either redemptive or adversarial: the activity and teaching together effecting at once a realisation of the eschatological rule of God and the rejection of Jesus that was to culminate in his death. I am not concerned here to decide between the various reasons proposed to explain why Jesus, as a matter of social and political fact, was put to death. Rather, the point is that whatever the particular causes, it was in some way his relations with his disciples, the people and the various authorities that shaped the way things happened. We are what we are, we experience the particular outcomes of our lives, in part because of the shape our relationships take with other people and the world. In that respect, Jesus was as we are, a creature in relations of 'horizontal' reciprocal constitution with other people and the world.

II 'Vertical' Relatedness

The inadequacies of any reductionist account, whether of Jesus or of ourselves, are compounded by the fact that any merely horizontal account of our being, however comprehensive in terms of scientific, social, historical and personal determinants, leaves out of the overall picture what we call the vertical dimension of our createdness. The word creature means, at least it used to mean, the product of the personal agency of God. In the second part of the lecture, I wish to explore equally briefly what it means to be in a network of relationships that includes relatedness to God. There are three dimensions, corresponding to the threefold tensing that we met in the New Testament accounts of Jesus. So far as the past is concerned, the doctrine of creation holds that the world and all it contains comes from the free creative act of God. That divine freedom is the chief burden of the doctrine of creation out of nothing, as Irenaeus makes so clear in his dispute with the Gnostics. Our past, those parts of the world from which we are made and to which we relate, comes from God. We come from nothing, in the sense that but for our calling into being by the love of God, we should not be. What might be called the existential point of the doctrine is, to cite Luther's famous words: 'that I should believe that I am God's creature, that he has given me a body, soul, good eyes, reason, a good wife, children, fields, meadows, pigs and cows. . . . Thus this article teaches that you do not have your life of yourself, not even a hair.'[6] In other words, the doctrine of creation teaches a form of gracious ontological dependence coming from our past.

The use of a present tense, of a doctrine of conservation or preservation, is that the ontological dependence is not merely a matter of past determination, from which everything else flows by some logical necessity, but a continuing relationship of dependence upon a personal God. We continue to be because we are

---

6. Martin Luther, 'Sermons on the Catechism, 1528,' in *Martin Luther. Selections from his Writing*, edited with an introduction by John Dillenberger, New York: Anchor Books, 1961, pp. 208f.

in a particular relationship with God. If that relationship ceased, so should we, just as all life on the earth would be instantaneously extinguished were the sun to disappear. Past creation and present conservation are what can be called, after Barth, two moments of creaturely dependence upon the creator.

It is in relation to both the past and present tenses of creation that the question of sin must be raised. The doctrine of original sin holds that somewhere in the past of the human race—and here we are not bound, if we wish to maintain the truth of the doctrine, to hold to a belief either in the literal story of Adam or in the form the doctrine of sin has often taken in the past—there took place a determination of the human race to a disrupted or disorderly relation to the God from whom it takes its being. Because for human beings the relation to the creator is personal—one, that is, between free beings who exist in relation to each other—it can take the form of orientation to life or to death. Insofar as original sin holds sway, the deathwards direction of life holds the upper hand: there is a determination towards dissolution. On the other hand, the doctrine of actual sin—the present tense of the doctrine—teaches that all human beings have their being in a network of disrupted relations between the human race and God—in structures shaped by original sin—so that as a matter of fact apart from redemption, they are able to replicate only the patterns of disorder.

The nature of the human creature, however, cannot be understood without attention also to the third of the three tenses. Very early in the Christian tradition, the doctrine of creation was given a teleological or eschatological orientation. Creation was not simply the making of the world out of nothing, not even that world continually upheld by the providence of God, but the making of a world destined for perfection, completedness. To be a creature means to be

a being called and directed to a future perfection. Those
who first proclaimed that the chief end of man is to
glorify God and enjoy him for ever enunciated a
profound truth. I should like to add that this eschatology should contain an additional reference to the world
which forms the context for that human calling. Not
only are we called to give our souls and bodies as a
living sacrifice of praise to our creator, but along with
them the whole creation, represented as it is in the
sacramental elements of water, bread and wine.

And that leads into a theme that will dominate the
rest of the lecture. It is a feature of Christian eschatology, much neglected in the past with its tendency to a
dualistic separation of this world and the world to
come, that the conditions of the age to come may be
anticipated in this one. The agent of such anticipation is
the Holy Spirit, understood, in St. Basil's expression, as
the perfecting cause of the creation: 'the original cause
of all things that are made, the Father; . . . the creative
cause, the Son; . . . the perfecting cause, the Spirit.'[7]
Through the Holy Spirit the bread and wine may
become the body and blood of the Lord, the Christian
church from time to time the community of the last
days, and the colour painted by the artist the truth of
the creation. If we are to understand the nature of the
humanity of Jesus, it will be by attention to the part the
Holy Spirit plays in his life, ministry, death, resurrection and ascension. And so we return to christology.

III *Episodes in a Narrative Particularity*

Jesus, we have seen, is a creature in the sense that his
life like our lives took shape in patterns of horizontal
relatedness with others and with the world. That is the

---

7. Basil of Caesarea, *On the Holy Spirit*, XV. 36

way in which he is of one substance with ourselves, a human creature. However, when the New Testament presents the humanity of Jesus, it shows him to be also in certain respects in a different relation from ours to both God and the network of created relationships. In the latter case, he is portrayed as being in a relationship that must be called redemptive. As bound up with the world as any other human being, he is yet its lord and redeemer, recalling it from its bondage to decay so that it may participate in its true directedness. The distinctiveness of the former relationship is that, without prejudice to his Jewish humanness, he is related in particular ways to God the Father. In this lecture, I am concerned chiefly with those relationships that concern him as a human being, abstracting them, so far as is possible without distortion, from the ways in which, as eternal Son, he is related to the Father and to the world. That will be the burden of the next lecture.

Let me begin with what has been, until the modern age, and indeed, since early this century for Barth and those such as T. F. Torrance who have learned from him, the chief way in which to conceive the unique yet real humanity of Christ. The concepts of *anhypostasia* and *enhypostasia* express the way in which the *person* of Christ can be understood in relation, on the one hand, to history and creation and, on the other, to God. *Anhypostasia* does not teach, as is sometimes alleged, the impersonality of Christ's humanity, but the fact that his hypostasis, his person, does not have its basis in the way that ours do in the processes of the finite world alone. What he does receive from the common basis of life we shall examine later, but we are already warned against the evolutionary reductionism that would in some way base his full significance in cosmic or historical processes. I mentioned earlier an agreement with the christology of John Robinson. Where agreement ceases is with his apparent belief that Jesus'

evolutionary past is enough to account for his full
significance. There is a suspicion in Robinson's book,
and in some of the things Rahner says, of a deification
of the evolutionary process, so that it rather than the
free and transcendent God takes the initiative in what
happens. Anhypostasia guards against any such deification. *Enhypostasia*, on the other hand, supplements
the negative—*not* the same basis as our persons—with a
positive: that the person of Christ—his unitary historic
being—has its basis in the Son and in the new act of
Father in him. It follows that Jesus' humanity is the
humanity of the eternal Son. Jesus is the eternal Son
become incarnate.

So far, so good. If modern Christianity is to retain
its integrity as gospel, something of this kind is
essential. In Jesus we meet God redemptively present
to the world in person. Apart from that, the gospel is
void, and we seek salvation in some immanent process
rather than the free grace of God. But there are
problems. The first is that, as it stands, the doctrine of
the *enhypostasia* is patient of interpretations that effectively deny the humanity of Jesus. Recently, I have
become convinced that this may well be the outcome of
the use of the concept by Karl Barth. To say that the
person is the person of the Son, or even that it is
established in its humanity as the humanity of the Son,
does not of itself guard against the threat of a
swallowing up of the humanity in the divine action. It is
worth pausing here to examine what happens in Barth's
treatment of the humanity of Christ. Because the
humanity of Christ is for Barth the humanity of God,
everything that happens is for Barth the act of God.
That is right, but raises the question: in what sense is
everything that happens also the action and passion of
a man? That is a less easy question to answer on the
basis of Barth's writing, and brings us to the second
problem presented by the enhypostasia: that it cannot,

on its own, ensure a satisfactory treatment of the
episodic character of the narratives of Jesus' life, which
can so easily become telescoped in such a way that they
lose the significance of certain crucial episodes. The
doctrine of the humanity as the humanity of the Son
can, unless supplemented by counterweights, too
easily overlook the importance of certain episodes in
which the free human activity of Jesus needs to be duly
expressed.

   Two examples can be given of what happens. The
first is Augustine's teaching that Jesus cannot have
received the Holy Spirit at his baptism, because he must
have had the Spirit all the time.[8] This is in danger of
suggesting that the Spirit in some way predetermines
all that Jesus does, a kind of automatic pilot. There is
little doubt that much Christian teaching over the
centuries has fallen into the fault of suggesting an
unreal humanity, and thus far the modern preoccupation with 'the historical Jesus' and the reality of his
experience is justified. The second example is provided
by a recent contrast of the christology of Barth and
Anselm. Dr. Gordon Watson has argued that by virtue
of his identification of revelation and atonement as
divine action, Barth is able to appreciate neither
Anselm's stress on the part played in the atonement by
the freedom of Jesus nor Kierkegaard's parallel stress on
the centrality of faith. '(W)e may ask of Barth whether
his criticisms of St Anselm's presentation do not reveal
a tendency in his theological method of raising to
understanding the particularity of the humanity of
Jesus' life-act through its direct association with the
inconceivable act in which God posits himself, that is,

---

8. Augustine, *De Trinitate* XV. 46: 'It would be utterly absurd for us
to believe that he received the Holy Spirit when he was already thirty
years old . . . but (we should) believe that he came to that baptism both
entirely sinless and not without the Holy Spirit.'

to convert the contingency and relativity of creaturely being into an aspect of an all-encompassing idea.'[9]

The weaknesses of the *enhypostasia* teaching are alleviated, if not removed, if we give a more prominent place than has been the case to the place of the Holy Spirit in christology. It is surely relevant here to note that the deficiencies of the Western tradition in its treatment of pneumatology, beginning with Augustine and culminating in Barth, are of a piece with its failure to do justice to the humanity of Christ. We must then ask: If the Holy Spirit is the eschatological perfecting cause of the creation, what must we say in the light of such teaching of the human career of Jesus? In the terms of our earlier discussion, we recall that the Spirit is the bearer of the third tense of createdness: of the creation's directedness to its perfection in God. The distinctive work of the Spirit is, through Christ, to perfect the creation. The function of the Spirit in relation to Jesus is, accordingly, as the perfecter of his humanity. Just as the *enhypostasia* reminds us of the origin of our salvation in the eternal love and action of God, so attention to the Holy Spirit reminds us of the way in which the saving action of Jesus is accomplished humanly in time. Too much stress on either can lose essential dimensions of the gospel.

Let us look, in this light, at episodes in the life of Jesus as they are presented in the gospels. First, a discussion of the beginning of Jesus' life, as it has been dogmatically expounded with the help of the doctrine of the virgin birth. Over the centuries, this doctrine has been used for a number of incompatible purposes: either to shield Jesus from the pressures and challenges of our being—preprogrammed humanity, so to speak

---

9. Gordon Watson, 'A Study in St. Anselm's Soteriology and Karl Barth's Theological Method,' *Scottish Journal of Theology* 42 (1989) pp. 493–512 (pp. 511f).

—or to express his total involvement in them. The former is achieved most completely by doctrines of the immaculate conception, which ensure Jesus' sinlessness by excluding him completely from the soil of sinful earth. He can be the redeemer only if his perfection is guaranteed in advance, only, that is, if his flesh is in effect that of unfallen Adam. Similar in outcome, though with opposite intent, is Barth's treatment of the virgin birth. At the centre of Barth's concern is to hold that at the beginning of Christ's earthly life, as at the end, there is a miracle, a new divine initiative, a mystery of revelation. That is true and important. In so far as the coming of Christ is the incarnation of the one through whom the world was made, it represents a new beginning, a renewal of the soiled and lost creation. But is not the effect of this still to overstress the divine action *towards* the creation at the expense of that action *within* the structure of time and space? It is in this context that Barth speaks of '(revelation's) character as a fact in which God has acted solely through God and in which likewise God can be known solely through God . . .'.[10] What is happening within the creation receives less attention, because Barth is unable to specify an action of the Spirit except in terms of 'God Himself in His freedom exercised in revelation to be present to His creature.'[11] The problem with Barth's account is not what he says, but what he fails to say. What he misses is precisely the specific action of the Spirit as the one enabling the creation truly to be itself.

In the development of this theme, any tritheistic suggestion that there are independent actions by each of the persons of the Godhead must be avoided. To quote Irving, whom I wish to use as a counterweight to

---

10. Karl Barth, *Church Dogmatics* I/2, E.T. edited by G. W. Bromiley and T. F. Torrance, Edinburgh: T & T Clark, 1956, p. 177.
11. Barth, p. 198.

Barth here, 'The Holy Ghost worketh nothing of Himself, but worketh the common pleasure of the Father and the Son. In the creation, therefore, of this body of Christ of the woman's substance, there is an act of the Father's will and a word of the Son assenting thereto'.[12] Yet there is a reason for attributing a specific dimension of the action to the Spirit. Irving uses the fact that Jesus is formed in the womb of Mary by the Holy Spirit to show that he is indeed part of the network of creation, in all its fallenness. By forming a body for the Word in the womb of Mary, the Spirit shows that the being of the human Jesus is not merely the passive object of the eternal Son's determination: it is also flesh of our flesh, bone of our bone. That is the point of denying that Jesus bore the flesh of unfallen Adam. If he did, what is his *saving* relation to us in our lost-ness?

One chief function of the doctrine of the virgin birth is accordingly to say something about Jesus' humanity, and thus to place him in a particular way at the intersection of the horizontal and vertical dimensions. He is indeed part of the created order, and although his humanity is that of the Son, it is no less than ours part of the general network and relationality of created being—and that means being on the way to dissolution in meaninglessness. It is from the same network in which we share that the body of the Son is formed. If, in correspondence to this, we understand the Spirit as the Father's 'second' hand, over against the world, enabling it to be itself—to be perfected—we shall see the importance of this dimension. In shaping from the clay of earth a body for the Son, the Spirit enables *this* part of earth to be fully itself, to move to perfection rather than to dissolution. In sum, then, we can say that

---

12. Edward Irving, *The Collected Writings of Edward Irving*, edited by G. Carlyle, London: Alexander Strahan, 1865, volume V, p. 122.

the point of the doctrine of the virgin birth is not to 'prove' the divinity of Christ, but to link together divine initiative and true humanity. Jesus is within the world as human, and yet as new act of creation by God.[13]

We come now to the second major stage of the human life of Jesus, the baptism and temptation, which for the purposes of this discussion we shall take as a single episode with a number of aspects. This, too, is something rather neglected by the tradition, which has to that extent merited the charges of docetism often levelled at orthodox christology. The baptism has long been taken by the Orthodox tradition as a revelation of the being-in-relation that is the Trinity: the Father acknowledges the Son and sends the Spirit. But it is important also to realise its significance for the *human* saviour. The Spirit directs the life of Jesus in one way rather than another. Just as the birth involved him in the network of human relatedness, so the baptism anoints him for a ministry to Israel, the people of God under judgement. As anointed, he is therefore brought into relation with Israel through his exercise at once of the three great offices of Israel: as prophet, priest and king. Before, however, we move to a treatment of them, some attention must be given to that with which they are inextricably bound, the trial of the calling which is the temptation.

The general human relevance of the temptation narratives is clear. If Jesus did not share our human trials, he is as irrelevant to our needs as if he had not borne the same flesh. That he did, shows, according to

---

13. It is worth referring here to the distinction drawn by Edward Irving between the *person* of Christ and the *nature* he bore. The person is indeed enhypostatic, the person of the Word, and therefore continuous, in a way we shall examine, with eternity. But the nature he takes on is continuous with ours, and, being taken from the network of the interrelated order of creation cannot but participate in its fallenness. It is the function of the Holy Spirit to enable the incarnate Jesus to bear that flesh through life, purify it and offer it perfect to the Father.

the verse of the Letter to the Hebrews cited in the first lecture, that he is of some assistance to those who are tempted now. Yet modern theology, for all its stress on the importance of Jesus' humanity, has often failed to come to terms with the dogmatic implications of the theme. According to Schleiermacher, to take one important example, Jesus can have experienced no real conflict or temptation if he was to be truly the perfectly religious man.

> . . . His development must be thought of as free from everything which we have to conceive as conflict . . . Thus at every moment of his period of development He must have been free from everything by which the rise of sin in the individual is conditioned.[14]

According to Irving, writing about the same time, the opposite was true. To bear fallen human flesh is necessary if Jesus is to complete the work to which he was called. What is important soteriologically was that Jesus was enabled to resist temptation not by some immanent conditioning, but by virtue of his obedience to the guidance of the Spirit. Irving argues that it is indeed necessary to salvation to believe:

> that Christ's soul was held in possession by the Holy Ghost, and so supported by the Divine nature, as that it never assented unto an evil suggestion, and never originated an evil suggestion: while on the other hand His flesh was of that mortal and corruptible kind which is liable to all forms of evil suggestion and temptation, through its participation in a fallen nature and fallen world.[15]

---

14. F. D. E. Schleiermacher, *The Christian Faith*, translated by H. R. Mackintosh and J. S. Stewart, Edinburgh: T & T Clark, 1928, pp. 382f.
15. Irving, *Writings* V, pp. 126f.

But to that general point must be added the particular one that the temptations are not temptations that would befall most of us in that form, because they are those consequent upon the calling that follows from the divine acknowledgement and the sending of the Spirit. They are consequent upon Jesus' baptism, or, we might say, upon a calling to be the messiah of Israel. The temptations are messianic: suggestions to choose one kind of course—what might be called a worldly course—rather than another. The replies placed on the lips of Jesus express his response in terms of what I have called his vertical relatedness. For him, the relation to God the Father, revealed at baptism, requires a particular response, of free worship and obedience.

The question of freedom is here a very important one. (We have seen that according to one commentator, Barth was unable to incorporate into his theology the teaching of Anselm on the free obedience of Jesus). In the modern world, we often speak as if freedom is an absolute, something that a human being just has. But as the Augustinian tradition rightly holds, insofar as we sin, we are deprived of the capacity to act freely. Had Jesus, hypothetically, succumbed to the temptations to be a political messiah—and we must be able to make the supposition if the temptations are to be a reality—he would have lost his freedom. In remaining true to the demands of his calling, he thus establishes his freedom. But there is a more important and positive matter at stake when we talk of Jesus' freedom. The positive dimension of his freedom is that he accepts it as gift from the Father's sending of the Spirit. Freedom is not an absolute, but something exercised in relation to other persons, and that means in the first instance that it is the gift of the Spirit who is God *over against us,* God in personal otherness enabling us to be free. It is in our relatedness that we are free or not, and this is true for all human life, as we shall see in the fourth lecture,

where we shall learn that the link between Jesus'
freedom and ours is to be found in the work of the Holy
Spirit.

But that is to anticipate. Here, our task is to
understand the particular way in which Jesus exercised
his freedom in relation to God. Our quest will be aided
if we follow up a little what has been made in the
tradition of the Old Testament background to the idea
of messiahship. It was long observed that in the Old
Testament there are three typical forms of messiahship,
in its etymologically original sense of a being anointed:
to be a prophet, a priest or a king. The tradition, and
particularly that of the Reformation, has made much of
the fact that Jesus acts as all of these. A reading through
Luke's account of the temptations and their aftermath
will make it evident that here we have a prophet and
king: the one who emerges from the wilderness—'in
the power of the Spirit' (Luke 4:14)—speaks the truth
and has authority over the creation, healing its sick-
nesses. But, it seems to me, the possibilities for
understanding Jesus' relation to the creation are greater
if, without denying the importance of those two, we
concentrate attention on what he does, through the
empowering of the Spirit, as priest. In doing this, we
shall move towards a discussion of the third area of his
human life with which we are here concerned, his
passion and subsequent death.

Irving argued, appealing to Acts 2 and Hebrews 5,
that it is only after the resurrection that Jesus was
anointed with his priestly power and authority. Only
then is he the one who is able to pour out on others the
Holy Spirit that had led him through his life.[16] Behind
that claim, there is an important insight, that Jesus'
relation to the Spirit changes as a result of his
glorification. It enables us to particularize different

16. Ibid., p. 236f.

aspects of his humanity in a way that a christology of *enhypostasia* alone does not. Despite this, however, I believe that it would involve a narrowing if we were so to limit the priestly function of Christ. There is also an important sense in which there are to be discerned in the baptism and temptations the beginnings of a priestly activity, not of mediating the Spirit of the Father to humankind, but the *human* priestly action of offering to the Father the perfection of a true human life. In support, we can appeal to one of the few direct allusions that the author to the Hebrews makes to the Holy Spirit, that Christ 'through the eternal Spirit offered himself without blemish to God . . .' (Heb 9:14). That is a priestly act, and it enables us to say that Jesus' particular humanity is perfected by the Spirit, who respects his freedom by enabling him to be what he was called through his baptism to be. That sacrificial offering can be understood in its fullness if it is seen to consist not only in the life laid down, but in the whole pattern of a life leading to passion and death.

What does this tell us of Christ's relation to the creation? I suggested above that, eschatologically considered, to be the creation is to be that whose directedness is to a future perfection before God. In the perfect offering of himself to the Father through the eternal Spirit we witness one sample—and Irving can even speak of this as a *random* sample—of the creation in its integrity. By virtue of its fallenness, the rest of the creation has lost its integrity, lost its directedness to perfection before God the Father. Though directed to an end which is perfection for the glory of God, the creation has, unaccountably but undoubtedly, fallen into disorder: that is to say, misdirection, disorientation and dissolution. One chief metaphor through which the misdirection can be understood is that of a deep-seated pollution, as the result of which everything participates in a unfittedness to go into the presence of the holy

God. The metaphors of dirt and pollution enable us to speak concretely of a disorientation of relations both vertical—in relation to God—and horizontal—in relation to the network of created reality.[17] At the centre of the disorientation of relations is the human creature, which, because of the personal and culpable form of its sin, involves all other reality in its fallenness. Both literally and metaphorically to be fallen is to pollute and to be polluted.[18] It is therefore appropriate that the first fruits of redemption should be the free, obedient and loving self-offering of this true human life to God the Father.

We now come to the third episode in the career of Jesus to which I wish to call attention. It is his death. The stress on the part played by God the Spirit in relation to the birth, baptism, temptation and all the subsequent episodes of the life of Jesus—those outlined in the account of the gospel teaching in the previous lecture—enables us to provide the context for a theology of the cross, the end to which the priesthood of Jesus is directed from the very beginning. As the completion of the pattern of the life, the cross is the outcome of the two marks of Jesus' humanity as we have described them: of the involvement of the incarnate Son in the network of the fallen creation and of his obedience to the Father's will worked out in the temptations and ministry. The relation of the human Jesus to the creation is therefore describable as a saving one. What he achieves, freely because through the enabling of the Spirit, is a matter of redemption because he offers to God the Father, through the Spirit, a

---

17. For an elaboration, see Colin E. Gunton, *The Actuality of Atonement*, chapter 5.

18. That is not to imply that all evil is caused by or in some way the fault of the human race, but that sin is at once the worst evil—in destroying both the soul and the body—and that it involves all other reality into itself.

renewed and cleansed sample of the life in the flesh in which human being consists.

In that respect, contrary to Barth's picture, the miraculous birth of Jesus belongs dogmatically more with the temptation and cross than with the resurrection, for it is the beginning of the human story that moves to the cross ('and a sword shall pierce through your own soul also', Luke 2:35). When we recall that it is the specific work of the Spirit to enable the created world to be itself, we can understand that, as we see in the conception of Jesus the Father's initiation through the Spirit of a new creation, so the cross is the place where Jesus, through the Spirit, perfected the obedience that he had learned through his temptation and ministry. His death is the shape that obedience must necessarily take in a fallen world, a world disordered by disseminated corruption. But his obedience is salvific because here we have a representative sample of fallen flesh purified and presented to God the Father. The sample is representative in standing for the rest of the created order, in due time to be taken up into the recapitulation there accomplished. Of that, more in the final lecture.

IV A Threefold History

The fourth and fifth episodes are the resurrection and ascension. I introduce them by saying that, like the cross, they can in different ways be said to be historical events which end the life of Jesus. To understand them we must realise the different senses in which this is so. The cross ends his life in the most public sense, but also in the most straightforwardly historical sense of the word 'event'. We have seen something of what it means for Christ the creature to end his life by dying. But in another sense, the life is not yet ended. The cross is indeed a kind of completion, a full and perfect sacrifice. But it is not the last word, which remains that of the one whose will was done in Jesus' ministry and death. We must therefore proceed by saying something also of how it comes about that this random sample of the creation comes into relation with the rest of the fallen world. Establishing the relation is one function of the doctrines of the resurrection of Jesus of Nazareth from the dead and of his ascension in glory to the side of the Father. If we pursue the matter with the aid of the two metaphors we have employed before, we can say, without in any way wanting so to restrict the distinction between those two events, that the resurrection is to be understood chiefly in terms of Jesus' horizontal relations with the created order, the ascension of primarily vertical relations. At the same time, however, we shall stress that both of the events, being what they are, relativize the distinction between vertical and horizontal, because they are events that open up earth to heaven and heaven to earth. But let us first examine them in turn.

We have already seen the resurrection to perform three functions according to the New Testament: of establishing the universality and exemplary character of the person of Christ, and of promising a completion to his story. We now explore the dogmatic and ontological ramifications of its affirmation. What is changed in Jesus' relationality by virtue of the resurrection? At the heart of the matter is the affirmation that the risen Jesus is brought into some kind of constitutive relation with all creation. If the resurrection is an event which universalizes the relation of the historical Jesus of Nazareth to the world, it must therefore at least in large measure be understood in terms of what we have called the horizontal relationality of Jesus. That, for example, is certainly the implication of the biblical passages we examined in the previous lecture. I Corinthians 15, for example, is a theology of the resurrection touching the rule of the risen Jesus over the world. Similarly, it is clear from the gospels that, for the most part, Jesus saw that it was in his relations with the chosen people of God that his calling consisted. What the resurrection does is to extend those relations universally. Here, if anywhere we may speak of retroactive force. The resurrection brings it about that this man is not just for and against Israel, the mediator of her salvation and judgement, but that his eschatological rule is universal.[19] It follows that the mission of those who affirm the resurrection is now to proclaim the eschatological judgement on all things of the crucified and risen Jesus.

But such a claim involves us in further ontological enquiry, for we have seen that one feature the different accounts of the resurrection have in common is their implication that the flesh of Jesus is transformed into the conditions of the age to come. This means that the perfection promised for the creation and realised through the work of the Spirit is centred here. It is for this reason essential that we reject all subjectivist and Bultmannian interpretations of the resurrection. The view, most recently associated, rightly or wrongly, with the Bishop of Durham that the gospel is to do with personal or existential transformation only, and not with the bodily and cosmic, is not only inadequate exegesis of scripture but effectively restricts the possibilities of conceiving a transforming relationship between Christ and the whole creation. Yet if we recall the lordship of Christ as depicted in the gospels, it is one consisting in a reassertion of the rule of God over the

---

19. It is in relation to this theme that the question of the relation of Jesus to those who lived before him and those after him living and dying outside of the preaching of the gospel should be discussed. To proclaim the universality of Jesus is not to condemn to hell all those who do not respond to him. It is to leave to the mercy of God the means of the final realisation of the kingdom.

whole world. On such an understanding, the resurrection is indeed spiritual, where 'spiritual' means not personal or subjective but related to the Spirit's perfecting of all things through Christ. Something of what this means will be explored in the fourth lecture.

In this lecture, however, we are chiefly concerned to expound the character of Christ the creature and of his relations with creator and created. Our argument is advanced if we ask who it was raised Jesus from the dead. In one sense, that is a nonsensical question, for it is, and can only be, a triune act, the act of God, Father, Son and Spirit. All that happens is in every respect the action of the one God in dynamic and saving relation with the world. And yet the affirmation of the common activity of the triune God does not preclude, but, if we are to be true to scripture, requires the ascription, not merely the appropriation, of some acts as being peculiarly the work of particular persons. Incarnation and salvation must be understood as peculiarly the work of the Son if their implications for their place in the gamut of Christian doctrines is to be adequately understood. Similarly, the way the resurrection is construed trinitarianly makes some difference to its dogmatic implications. In his *Space, Time and Resurrection*, Thomas Torrance advocates an understanding of the resurrection not only as passive, but as the active 'taking again of the life that he had laid down,' so that the Son is conceived to raise himself from the tomb. Interestingly, Torrance bases the interpretation on the *enhypostasia*, and sees the resurrection as the completion of the active obedience that marks the life of the incarnate Son.[20] Unless, however, this is balanced by a firm assertion of the passivity of the Son, the link, made

---

20. Thomas F. Torrance *Space, Time and Resurrection*, Edinburgh: Handsel Press, 1976, p. 53.

so firmly in Paul between Jesus' resurrection, as the first
fruits, and ours is likely to be difficult to maintain.

Once again, there is need not only of christological
emphasis, but of pneumatological. As the one who
does the work of the Father in perfecting of creation, it
is the Spirit whom one would naturally see as the agent
of the eschatological act of resurrection taking place in
the midst of time. And it is precisely as first fruits of the
transformation of the whole creation that Jesus is
'horizontally' related to the of the world, as, to use the
familiar jargon, its future: as the arrhabon (2 Cor. 1:22),
down-payment, for what is to come. No wonder G. K.
Chesterton is to be found using this remarkable
rhetorical flourish at the close of a chapter on the
resurrection:

> On the third day the friends of Christ coming at day-
> break to the place found the grave empty and the stone
> rolled away. In varying ways they realised the new
> wonder; but even they hardly realised that the world
> had died in the night. What they were looking at was the
> first day of a new creation, with a new heaven and a new
> earth; and in the semblance of the gardener God walked
> again in the garden, in the cool not of the evening, but the
> dawn.[21]

Here we are able to make another important link in
a theology of the humanity of Jesus, between the new
creation that is his conception, the atonement as the
offering to God by Jesus of a representative sample of
fallen but perfected human flesh, and the resurrection
that achieves its eschatological perfecting. If the resurrection is to be more than a revelation of the meaning of
Christ and the will of the Father; if, that is to say, it is to

---

21. G. K. Chesterton, *The Everlasting Man*, London: Hodder and
Stoughton, 1925, p. 247.

do as well as simply *show* something, as the Bible suggests it does, then it is as the beginnings of an eschatological redemption that we must see it. (Hence, '(Jesus) was put to death for our sins and raised for our justification,' Rom. 4:25) The resurrection brings it about that the particular humanity of Jesus becomes the basis of universal redemption. Here, the pneumato-logical dimension is crucial. The one through whom the Father perfects the creation, by raising Jesus from the dead, makes Jesus the centre of the restoration of the fallen cosmos. The cosmos hereafter achieves its destiny in so far as it is gathered to him. This is in the first instance the redemption of the human creation, but involves other things in its relationality. As we have seen, we human creatures are the centre of the world's problems, and only by our redirection will the whole creation be set free.

It is in this context that we find the systematic placing of a number of other important theological themes: of the representative or vicarious nature of Christ's humanity, and of the related doctrine of the church as being his body or community. They are worth adumbrating here briefly because they show how the creatureliness of Christ bears upon the being and status of the rest of the creation. First, the resurrection establishes the representative status of Christ, because, as 'the first-born among many . . .', Rom 8:29, he becomes the means whereby, through the Spirit, other created reality becomes perfected. It is, as we have seen, a matter of relationality: of how the relations to God of this human life become throught the agency of the Spirit, the means of restoring to right relation those who had sought their own way and thus gone astray. Thus, second, the churchly dimension of the matter is shown by the fact that the Spirit, by relating his people to the Father through the crucified and risen Jesus, moves towards perfection those first created in the image and likeness of their maker. Something of how that comes about, of how the creation is restored to God, through Christ and in the Spirit, as an act of God as well as of the human Jesus, will be the theme of the next lecture.

In this one, however, we come now to the third phase of the 'ending' of Jesus' story, and the fifth of the episodes with which we are concerned, the ascension. It is clear that this is a 'historical' event in an even odder sense than is the resurrection. The latter, as Pannenberg has demonstrated, can be illuminated, if not very adequately expounded, by exploring its reports with the tools of modern historiography. (One wonders how much Pannenberg is playing a rather old-fashioned evidential game with his interpretation of the resurrection.)[22] Even less will be learned of the ascension, even though it can be claimed to be historical in the sense that it is something that happened in time, as the final closure of Jesus' earthly career. What it clearly involves is the taking up of his humanity into God.

Does this mean that there has always been a 'humanity of God', as the later Barth argued? I think that we should be chary of that kind of speculation about the inner being of deity. Clearly, both incarnation and resurrection imply a capacity of God for relatedness to the created world. But whether we should speculate further is doubtful in view of the danger of a mythologizing of the historical. What is not in question is the acknowledgement of Jesus as the mediator of the ways of the eternal with the world, and it undoubtedly entails that the ascension is the revelation of something that is true eternally. But in terms of the economy of salvation, of the ways of God to the world, what must be emphasized is that here is not merely revelation, but

---

22. Wolfhart Pannenberg, *Jesus—God and Man*, translated by L. L. Wilkins and D. A. Priebe, London: SCM Press, 1968, pp. 88–106.

event, something which brings about a new state of affairs. History is decisive. What is changed is, indeed, the relation of Jesus to God in the sense that he is taken up into the eternity of the Godhead, and 'lives ever to make intercession' for his people. But should we not understand this chiefly in terms of the economy of salvation, of the ways of God to the world, rather than in some way that might appear to suggest a change in the inner being of God?[23]

The point of the ascension, to repeat what was said in the first lecture, is that it represents a bridge between heaven and earth, a ladder to heaven. The ascension of Jesus is concerned to bring out the character of the mediation that he represents and is. It is also concerned to bring out the inadequacy of the spatial metaphors which are so plentiful and dangerous in christology: of above and below, of vertical and horizontal relationships, of ladders to heaven. There is indeed, 'a way for man to rise to that sublime abode': but it is through the risen and ascended Christ. The ascension is often treated as little more than an appendix to talk of the resurrection, as for example in Barth's treatment of virgin birth and resurrection as miracles to mark the

---

23. Again, in connection with the question already raised of the sense in which the resurrection can be spoken as having retro-active force, it can be suggested that the discussion is better held in connection with the ascension, for it is this that relates Jesus newly to the Father and so realises for all the world the work of Christ. To say, as Pannenberg appears to do, ibid., pp. 135–141, that the resurrection is an event which *realises* the oneness of Jesus with God is not only to produce logical contortions, to appear to say that before the resurrection he was not uniquely one with the Father, but that after it he is made to have been one with him all along; but it also appears to rule out the pneumatological dimensions that have been stressed in this lecture. Is not the Holy Spirit the one by whom we understand Jesus to have been from the beginning one with the Father? Pannenberg's is a characteristically Western christology in failing to give constitutive significance to the part played by the Holy Spirit in the life and ministry of Jesus. But it is also characteristically immanentist—the result of the same pneumatological weakness—in failing to distinguish adequately between what I have called horizontal and vertical relationality.

beginning and end of Jesus' earthly life. Yet here we have what can be more appropriately be seen as the closure than can the resurrection, in that it is the ascension that establishes Jesus as the eternal mediator between heaven and earth, by virtue of that which he did and suffered as a man. As the resurrection opens the creation upwards to the holy God, so the ascension completes what comes first, the earthwards movement of the Son, the opening of heaven to earth.

V Transition

I have begun the dogmatic as distinct from the exegetical phase of the lectures with a treatment of Christ the creature for a number of reasons. One is to concede the moment of truth in the claim made by exponents of christology from below that we may not begin in the heavens, and move thence to earth, but must in some way or other earth our christology in the historical Jesus. Christology is bound to begin with Jesus. That is right, but there is a qualification to be made. We may not build our own ladder to heaven, so that the Jesus with whom we begin is not our own invention or discovery. It is of the essence not only of our creaturehood but of its fallenness that we are unable to approach the holy God apart from his initiative. To be sure, there is need of mediation, but in view of the human condition it must be provided by God. That is the point of christology, of the confession that in Jesus it is not merely a man but the eternal God who meets us.

On what, then, may we base an affirmation that here we have not merely a creature, but also and without detriment to his creatureliness the incarnation of the eternal Son of God? In view of the fact that he does what he does as man, it is in some ways more by virtue of what happens to him than what he does as man that we make the affirmation. The content of the affirmation is, to be sure, that *all* that Jesus does and suffers is the work of the Father through the Spirit, and therefore the action and passion of the divine Son. But the reason we make it is not because it is in some way evident or demonstrable 'from below', but because God the Father through the Holy Spirit makes it knowable—reveals to us—that the whole is his work and will. In the next lecture, we shall move to an examination of the content of the affirmation.

LECTURE 3

Incarnation, Kenosis and Divine Action

In the previous lecture, frequent use was made of the metaphorical terms, 'vertical' and 'horizontal' to characterize the relations of Jesus to God the Father on the one hand, and the world on the other. They are clearly metaphorical in the sense that God is not literally 'up there'. But are they necessary at all? Recent christology has seen many attempts to abandon them for a more generally horizontal picture: with the source of Jesus' significance rooted in some way either in history or the cosmos. Christologies with an orientation to evolution will thus locate the divine activity that emerges in Jesus of Nazareth in some way in past cosmic process;[1] while more eschatological christologies like Pannenberg's locate the weight of divine activity in the historical future, and continue to be chary of speaking too much of a movement 'from above'. The movement in his case is from the future, from the anticipated completion of historical process rather than from some supratemporal eternity.

---

1. J. A. T. Robinson, *The Human Face of God*, London: SCM Press, 1973; G. W. H. Lampe, *God as Spirit. The Bampton Lectures 1976*, London: SCM Press, 1977.

By shaping the direction of the lectures in the way
that I have, I have conceded something to the advocates
of christology from below, who are justified in their
suspicions that there is a docetic tendency in orthodox
christology. By virtue of its domination by treatments of
the divine Christ it has often failed to do justice to
Chalcedon's 'of one substance with ourselves'.[2] They
are also justified in their suspicion that ours is an
'immanentist' culture, and cannot easily come to terms
with apparently transcendentalist thinking. The point
of the previous lecture was to place the humanity of
Christ in the centre, and to generate a cosmology that is
relational rather than transcendental: with terms like
'vertical' and 'horizontal' avowedly metaphorical and
construed as making a distinction between relationships within and without the network of created reality.
Thus Christ in his incarnation is understood to be as
truly part of the created order as the rest of us, albeit in
importantly different relation to God. But there was no
intention by taking such an approach to deny the
classical doctrine. It is, after all, by the action of God
that the creation is restored to its true relation to God
and its due directedness. The time has therefore now
come to engage with the question of the way in which
that human activity has its roots in eternity, in the
eternal love of God: in other words, with traditional
forms of treatment of the divinity of Christ. For without
that dimension Jesus is of no interest except as an only
fairly exceptional historical person in our past.

---

2. I have argued elsewhere that the logic of most modern
christology 'from below' is in the direction of a worse docetism than
that alleged of the classical tradition. It is ironical that those who try
hardest to prove a christology on the basis of a human or historical
Christ find it most difficult in the end to establish the fullness of that
humanity. *Yesterday and Today. A Study of Continuities in Christology*,
London: Darton, Longman and Todd, 1983, chapter 2.

I Creation as Divine Action

The second lecture began with an outline of what it is to be a creature, and moved on from there to speak of the creatureliness of the incarnate Christ. In this lecture, I begin with a parallel treatment of creation. But there lies a problem. In one respect, the christological task is an easier one: there is, as we know, a tradition of speaking of Christ from the side of the creator. But in another way, it is more difficult. We are, after all, creatures, and while it may seem relatively unproblematic to reflect upon and produce theories of our creaturehood it is a very different matter to look at things from the other side, *sub specie aeternitatis.* Do we have privileged access to the inner life of God, that such a thing can be attempted? The scales seem to be loaded against us, and for two very important reasons. First, a broad range of modern thought has warned us against the attempt to probe beyond the phenomena. We cannot, it is said, penetrate below the surface appearances of things to find what is really there. That is especially true in the case of God. Second the theological tradition has also impressed upon us the impossibility and impropriety of seeking to describe the inner workings of deity. We are not given to know the constitution of God. Indeed, it is the charge of theological arrogance that underlies one of Pannenberg's objections to traditional christology.[3]

It is not possible in this lecture to give a detailed account of the reasons for refusing to accept the modern suspicion about knowledge beyond the surface appearances. The general considerations are that it is based upon a false view of the relation of person to world, of the nature and function of language and of the character of human knowing. Contrary to the modern

---

3. Wolfhart Pannenberg, *Jesus—God and Man*, translated by L. L. Wilkins and D. A. Priebe, London: SCM Press, 1968, p. 35.

suspicion, I believe that as those who indwell the world and are therefore continuous with it, as part of it, we are able to use both instruments and concepts as a way of relating to it and of articulating something of the being of things.[4] The second point, however, must be considered at greater length. What kind of knowledge of God is theologically legitimate, especially in connection with knowledge of God the creator? Can we really know anything of what it is to be God the creator? Much depends, I suggest, on what we mean by 'know.' If it is meant that we can in some way penetrate into the inner being and action of God, and describe what it means that he creates through the Son and Spirit, then we cannot claim to know. But there are other ways than that of knowing.

Let me begin with an extended analogy from the way in which we know ourselves. It is widely believed that we know ourselves by some form of introspection, as philosophers from Augustine through Descartes to many a modern have held. That, I believe, is the least reliable form of knowledge, for reasons which cannot be reviewed here. Instead, I put an alternative. In the previous lecture I argued to a theology of being from structures of relations. Who we are is made known to us through the relations in which we stand. There are three forms of relation that can be abstracted from the overall network: relations with the world, with other human persons and with God. Those relations reveal different ranges of mutuality and reciprocity, but they all, and especially the third, provide us with mirrors in which we may see ourselves as we are.

The way in which, first, we know ourselves through our relations with other human beings is

---

4. For arguments in support of the view I here take, see my *Enlightenment and Alienation. An Essay Towards a Trinitarian Theology,* London: Marshall, Morgan and Scott, 1985.

relatively straightforward. We know ourselves as we observe the affect that we have on them, and they on us. (This is clear from the moral insensitivity often shown by those who are blind to the effect they have on others. They do not know themselves because they are unconscious of the reactions of others to their actions.) While such relations reveal, despite considerable differentiation, something approaching symmetry, this is not the case with the second class of relations, those with the non-personal world. The non-personal world is subordinate in the sense that it requires the world of persons if it is to be truly itself; that is the point of the God-given human dominion over the creation. And while it is not entirely passive in relation to our agency—however much we have vainly and sinfully tried to make it so—it is created in a relation of relative subordination. Yet, as we have seen, these relations also enable us to learn something of who and what we are. Through our agricultural, technical and artistic interactions with the world we come in part to know who we are.

But, third, it is our relations with God which concern us centrally in a study of the nature of creation. If we are creatures, then we take our being from the one who makes us what we are. If, however, we are *personal* creatures, our being manifests otherness and freedom in relations not only with each other, but with God. To be a person is to be a distinct and particular entity, albeit one whose being is constituted only through relatedness, and it is that most central feature of our being that can be known only by virtue of our relatedness with God. We come to know ourselves most surely as we see ourselves in varying relations with God, our creator and redeemer. (Underlying this claim is a belief in the necessity for revelation if we are to know who we are as creatures of God. The necessity is reinforced by the fact that as fallen creatures we can only know of our creatureliness as it is redeemed from dissolution. As Calvin argued, without the knowledge of God as our creator and redeemer, we are unable to know ourselves as we truly are.)

In sum, then, we know ourselves, we come to learn about the kind of beings that we are, as we live in terms of three different kinds of relations: as we live in the created world, with each other and before God our creator and redeemer. To ignore any of the three is to fail to know who and what we are. Yet it may be noticed—and this is the point of the extended analogy—that on such an account we make no claim to understand every aspect of what can be called the inner geography of our being. So, we may claim, is it with our knowledge of God. We come to a knowledge of God not by an improper probing into his inwardness, but by a consideration of the implications of his relatedness to the world. To put it simply: we know God because and as the Father comes into free relation with us and the world through his Son and Spirit.

It was by drawing out the implications of that simple teaching that the early church came, over centuries of debate, to formulate the doctrine of the Trinity. The implications for our understanding of God can be stated fairly simply. The one who is known by virtue of his free and personal relatedness to the world is one who is a relational being in himself. God, that is to say, is a communion: one who exists in the communion of Father, Son and Spirit: each with his own distinctive and particular being, yet all only what they are as a result of their relations in perichoresis with one another. It follows that God is personal, for to be a person is to exist in relations of free mutuality with other persons. Equally, it follows that God is love, for it is of the essence of love to exist through reciprocal giving and receiving. Finally, it follows that because God is love in advance—that is because there is already

personal relation-in-otherness within the divine communion—there is no need for God to create another. If
there is a creation, it flows from the free love of God,
from the inherent richness and many-sidedness of his
being, and not because of any need or lack in God
himself.

The next and fairly rapid step is what may appear
to be an outrageous generalisation: that the only
satisfactory account of the relation between creator and
creation is a trinitarian one. This is not to rule out of
consideration every aspect of all the theories of reality
to be found or implied in the philosophies, sciences and
religions of the world, but to hold that without a
trinitarian conceptualizing, accounts of creation are
deficient, and tend to collapse either, on the one hand,
into idealism, in which the (finally real) world is
understood as a projection of our individual or collec-
tive experience; or on the other into some some form of
pantheism, according to which the world is made into
the deity. The key to the matter is that of personal
relatedness, of the capacity for us to understand the
relation between God and the world as a matter of free
relatedness. It is because God the Father creates
through the Son and Spirit, his two hands (Irenaeus),
that we can conceive a world that is both real in itself,
and yet only itself in relation to its creator. (The
outcome of such a conception is a theology of the world
of the kind sketched in the previous lecture, as
constituting a structure of beings interrelated dynamically as a network of particularities in time and space.)

What, then, is the relation of the doctrine of the
Trinity to the christology that is here being developed?
Pannenberg has famously said, in the argument to
which I have already often referred, that the trouble
with traditional christologies is that they make the
mistake of presupposing the doctrine of the Trinity.
Rather, he holds, any doctrine of the Trinity must be

the outcome of christological thought. In a sense, the latter is true. A doctrine of the Trinity of the kind outlined above can only be the result of thought about the economy of salvation through Christ and the Spirit. That is the necessary order of knowing: from God's relatedness to the world, made known in Christ, to a doctrine of his eternal being in relation. But the order of being must take a different orientation. If there is to be talk of the incarnation, it must presuppose the existence of a triune God, for it holds that the one through whom the world was made has become part of that world in order to redeem it from its bondage to decay. In that respect, the two doctrines, of God and of Christ, offer each other mutual support, or, rather, are dependent upon one another. Without a presupposed Trinity, the doctrine of the incarnation becomes an absurdity. With it, the point of the doctrine of the Trinity comes to be further realised, for it can be understood that it is not absurd that the agent of creation, the one through relation to whom it comes to be, by whom it is held in being, and to whom it is directed, should so involve himself in what he has made.

As we have seen, the importance of a trinitarian understanding of the creation is that it makes it possible to distinguish between God and the world while also understanding them as being in relation. Let me spell out briefly the chief implications of this view for the development of a theology of Christ and creation. They would need far more detailed justification if this were a treatise on the Trinity or the doctrine of creation, but I am selecting only what we need for our purposes.[5] First, and centrally: that God creates the world through

---

5. Some of the detailed background to the very sketchy theology of these pages I have attempted in *The Promise of Trinitarian Theology*, Edinburgh: T & T Clark, 1991.

Christ, through the one who became flesh, implies that God is able to come into relation with the world while remaining distinct from it. It therefore bespeaks freedom in the relations of God to the world, something impossible in the Greek cosmology in the face of which the doctrine of the Trinity was first developed, for that tended to understand creation in a necessitarian way. And that takes me to the second point, which is that the doctrine of the Trinity enables us to conceive the relation of God to the world as a personal one. Because God is a being who is what he is in terms of free personal relatedness, he is not bound to come into relation with the world. But he can, freely, and therefore such relations as there are must be understood as unnecessitated relations of love. The incarnation is the climax and model of the free relatedness of the triune God to the world he has made and holds in being.

Third, the fact that creation is in the Spirit as well as through the Son enables us to say that it is not a timeless act, but that creation has a teleology, a direction. That is part of the point of the account of creation in six days. God creates freely, out of love: but it is a love that leaves the creature something to be and do: to live in time, to praise its creator and to return, perfected, to the one who made it. A full theology of creation, ordered in this way to christology and pneumatology, would require attention to be paid also to the way in which the misuse of human freedom disrupts alike the relation of the creature to God and the directedness of creation as a whole to its true end. But at this stage we are chiefly concerned with the way in which a trinitarian theology of creation enables us to conceive a world in open and dynamic relations with its maker.

In sum we can say this: that there is a history of relations between God and the world, so that the world

which *was* created can be understood now to take shape
in constant interaction with its creator and to be in
dynamic process towards its completion. It is thus that
we gain the conceptual equipment to speak of God's
relatedness to the world in the language of *involvement,
action, and enabling.* God's involvement derives from his
free relatedness to that which is not himself, grounded
in the creation of everything out of nothing. That
involvement cannot be understood without the concept
of action, for it is not the general involvement that is
expressed in pantheist and panentheist theologies.
Here something particular is achieved: there is brought
about that which, without the action, would remain
without being. But it is also an enabling, because by
that activity the world is given its own distinctive being
and through the Spirit empowered to be the world, and
not simply the tool or extension of deity. In this
connection what we call the history of salvation comes
to be conceived not in terms of divine interventions in a
world foreign to divine agency—the so-called laser-
beam theology—but the way by which God the Father,
through the work of the Son and the Spirit, maintains
and restores creation's directedness to perfection. Here,
as in the general matter of the relation of Trinity and
christology, there is mutual affect. Just as the doctrine
of the Trinity must necessarily be presupposed in
christology, and yet is in the outcome enriched by it, so
there is a mutual animation of the language of creation
and christology. The incarnation of the Son in time and
space has particular implications for an understanding
of God's relation to time, which then enable time and
space themselves to be newly conceived. So it is that
Thomas Torrance has argued that the christological
thinking of the Fathers enabled them to break free of
ancient views of space and time as a container,
externally related to God, and to generate in place of
them a relational view which enables a dynamic

interrelatedness of God and the world to come to expression.[6]

If, then, to be created is to be in indissoluble relation to God through the Son and Spirit, it follows that that shape of being, the dynamic form that it takes in its various space-time configurations, derives from creation's relation to its creator. Incarnation, the involvement of God the Son, on the initiative of the Father and through the enabling of the Spirit, then, is a violation of the being neither of God nor of the world. On the contrary, there is a sense in which it realises the true being of them both, for it perfects at once the Father's work of creation and the creature's determination to perfection. In the light of all this, let us look again at the traditional doctrine of the incarnation and its teaching of the coming of the one through whom all things were made into direct and personal relation with the creation.

II *Kenosis and Plerosis*

The doctrine of the incarnation states that, in obedience to the Father and through the perfecting action of the Spirit, the eternal Son comes in person to that realm which was made through him and which he continues to uphold. The 'creative' cause of the material world comes to his own: the one through whom creation was and is formed becomes part of the creation, without ceasing to be who he is eternally. In what takes place, the initiative is with the Father, so that all that happens is the will of the one from whom all things come and to whom they move. The Son and the Spirit are 'of one

---

6. Thomas F. Torrance, *Space, Time and Incarnation*, Oxford University Press, 1969.

substance with the Father', equal in divinity, but in the
economy do the Father's will as his 'two hands', the
agents of his creating and redeeming action in the
world. This giving of priority to the Father is not to take
away from the distinctive modes of action of the Son
and Spirit, but, on the contrary, to guarantee that full
weight is given to them.[7] This second section of the
lecture is, then, designed to show that a trinitarian
account of the relation of Christ and creation enables
due weight to be given both to God's otherness from
the world and to his saving action within it.

It is a commonplace of patristic theology that Jesus
Christ is the Word through whom all things were
created, made incarnate to restore and perfect the
creation. The latter phrase is of immense importance.
As Athanasius states, and Anselm repeats in slightly
different words, the purpose of the incarnation is to
prevent the good creation from failing to achieve its true
destiny: that the Father's intent of love should not fail
of its purpose.[8] In the first lecture, I said something
of the way in which the New Testament expresses this
through its conception of the cosmic Christ. In the
second lecture, something was added about the
achievement of the incarnate Son: as man, he begins a

---

7. That without it they lose their distinctive function is evident from
the 'modernist' christological movement, beginning with Schleiermacher, but taking English shape in the tradition stemming from *Lux
Mundi*, which tends to see the life of Jesus as in some way deriving from
the *movement* of history or the cosmos. In some recent British
christology, for example the writings of John Robinson and Geoffrey
Lampe cited in note 1, there is a tendency to locate the basis of the
incarnation—or what takes its place—in the processes of evolution. In
effect, this is to deify cosmic process, to make something created the
initiating source of what happens in the history of Jesus. It is also to
conceive the world as saving itself, and so renders the events with
which we are concerned little more than episodes in the evolution of
the cosmos.

8. Athanasius, *On the Incarnation* 6: 'For it were not worthy of God's
goodness that the things he had made should waste away . . .'. Cf.
Anselm *Cur Deus Homo* I:4.

restoration of creation's teleology by offering to the Father a true human obedience. In terms of the imagery of sacrifice, he effects the process of renewal by offering to the Father through the Spirit a cleansed and representative sample of the fallen flesh he bore through being born into a network of corruption. His resurrection attests and guarantees the eschatological perfection of that sacrifice.

We now turn to an account of the incarnation as an act of God. The point of the foregoing discussion has been to prepare the way conceptually for what is to come. That is because in an attempt to give some account of the affirmation that in the incarnation the eternal Son is wholly present within the structures of time and space it is largely conceptual matters with which we have to do. The reason is that we are not qualified to say, from an inside point of view, so to speak, how it happened that the Word became flesh, or, for that matter, in what sense it might be said that Jesus experienced divinity or was in some way conscious of being divine. The aim rather is to offer the best conceptual account we can of certain relationships. What is the character of the relationship to which we are pointed when the New Testament so clearly presents Jesus as at once eternal Son of the Father and yet fully man? As we have seen, there is on the whole no clear distinction drawn in scripture between what he is and does as man, and what as God. The concern is rather to show that his actions and the whole pattern of his life are presented as being on the two 'levels' at once. Theology's task is to express the meaning of this and its claim to truth conceptually in such a way that its implications for life and thought may become evident. What concepts may we then use to express as well as possible the claim that the Son becomes man while remaining God?

One indispensable concept is that of kenosis or

emptying, which suggests, following Philippians 2:7, that the eternal Son of God 'emptied himself, taking the form of a servant . . .'. The concept has a long and various history, and in its light two introductory points must be made. We must accept, in the first place, that we cannot call on the Letter to the Philippians in direct justification of later developments. There is in that passage the description of a divine-human action, but not a christological theory of any kind. The question we have to ask is whether it is right to develop the concept further, just as Irenaeus developed further the concept of recapitulation. Does the notion of kenosis enable us better to conceive what is happening in the life of Jesus? Second, we must beware of the use that has been made of the idea in some modern theology. The kenotic theory was developed to deal with a particular problem arising out of the encounter of the traditional patristic way of speaking of Jesus with the newly developing critical studies, which were insisting on the humanity, including the ignorance, of Jesus of Nazareth. The critical claims were causing to come home to roost matters that had long been evaded. One of the nettles—to mix the metaphor—that the Fathers had failed to grasp was that of the ignorance of Jesus. It was a commonplace for them to say that his expressions of ignorance were feigned.

For two reasons, we may not accept the commonplace. It flies in the face of the manifest witness of the scriptures and it fails to do justice to the orthodox teaching that Christ is fully human. It is part of the human condition to be finite and therefore limited in knowledge (although not, of course, to be sinful, which is a condition of fallen humanity). Modern kenotic theory derives from the way in which some, particularly Lutheran, theology met the challenge in the modern era. That theology, in distinction from the Reformed, had a strong teaching of the doctrine of the *communicatio idiomatum*: the teaching that anything which can be attributed to the humanity of Christ must also be attributable to his divinity, and vice versa. The humanity has the divine attributes, the divinity the human so that, for example if God is omniscient, then so must be the man Jesus. (Similarly, and here we can recognise the springs of the christology of Moltmann and, especially, Jüngel, if the man dies then so must we say that, in a sense, also does the God.) But critical studies were insisting on Jesus' manifest lack of omniscience and omnipotence.

A solution was attempted by a new use of the concept of kenosis. The theory came in many forms, but in general taught that at the incarnation the eternal Son in some way abandoned the use of those divine attributes which were apparently incompatible with his full humanity. At the incarnation, he emptied himself in the sense that he abandoned for a time some of the attributes of divinity. The difficulties of such a theory have been much rehearsed. The chief of them only needs to be repeated. If it is not God, one fully God, but a depotentiated divinity that meets us, then the gospel is void, for that holds that in Christ the fullness of the Godhead dwells bodily. 'God is always God even in his humiliation . . . . Any subtraction or weakening of it would at once throw doubt upon the atonement made in Him. He humbled Himself, but He did not do it by ceasing to be who He is.'[9] If this is salvation being achieved, then it must be the work of God himself, not of some mythical demi-god.

Such objection, however, does not deal a death blow to all use of the *concept* rather than theory of kenosis. If the self-emptying is seen as the *expression* of the divine being rather than its *depotentiation*, it is a

9. Karl Barth, *Church Dogmatics*, IV/1, edited by G. W. Bromiley and T. F. Torrance, Edinburgh: T & T Clark, 1956, pp. 179f.

different matter altogether. The concept is used, for example, in Cyril of Alexandria. 'The emptying was a voluntary reduction to our level, undertaken as an act of pure love . . . : "He who fills all things lowered Himself to emptying".'[10] What is claimed is that the eternal relatedness of the Son to the world here takes, through the Spirit, a particular and unique form. Because the Father created and upholds the world in being through the Son, it is ontologically appropriate, so to speak, for the Son to be the one who takes flesh. The one who holds in being the realms of time and space enters their confines in order to renew them. In that respect, the emptying is an expression at once of the love of the Son and of his being in relation with that which was created through and is upheld by him. Kenosis is therefore one concept by which we may express the way in which the eternal Son related himself to that which is not God—to the creation.

Accordingly we may say that the cross of Jesus represents the *fulfilment* of the self-*emptying* of the Son that takes form in the incarnation. That is only apparently a paradox, for the cross is no act of depotentiation. It is rather the supreme act of divine power: the power through which the world is made whole. Therefore we must say, following Forsyth, that the self-emptying is at the same time an act of fulfilment, of plerosis.[11] *Infinitum capax finiti*. In the incarnation the being of the Son expresses itself, is laid out in all its fullness, because in his self-emptying the Son is most fully divine. The eternal triune love of God takes historical shape in what is at once the sending by the Father, the Son's self-giving to death, and the enabling of the Spirit. In that sense, the self-emptying is

10. G. L. Prestige, *Fathers and Heretics*, London: SPCK, 1940, p. 165.
11. P. T. Forsyth, *The Person and Place of Jesus Christ*, London: Independent Press, 1909, Lecture XII.

in continuity with the act of creation, where too the love of God takes temporal and spatial form through the activity of Son and Spirit.

But it is doubtful whether the continuity between creation and incarnation should be expressed by calling the activity of divine creation also an act of kenosis. It is one thing to give to the world being and form, another to enter its fallen structures to renew them. The point of a concept like kenosis is that it enables us to pinpoint the significance of the incarnation, not that it should be applied elsewhere. There is a close logical link between kenosis and suffering, but little scriptural support for the view that to create is, for God, to suffer.[12] 'Creativity' may cause *us* suffering, and probably should be expected to, but that is because human agency takes form in and towards a fallen world. Biblical accounts of creation, however, tend to stress not suffering, but freedom and joy: 'when the morning stars sang together, and all the sons of God shouted for joy', Job 38:7. God sees all that he has made, and it is very good.

The continuity of redemption with the act of creation is not therefore best expressed by the concept of kenosis, which concerns rather the shape God's saving involvement in *fallen* time and space must necessarily take. Creation is not kenosis. Yet the kenosis is none the less a plerosis because here the eternal being of the Son takes historical shape in incarnation and cross. Kenosis, accordingly, is an appropriate concept to use in christology insofar as it enables us to show something of how it is that

---

12. Jürgen Moltmann, *God in Creation. An Ecological Doctrine of Creation*, translated by Margaret Kohl, London: SCM Press, pp. 86–93. There is a thin line between, on the one hand, maintaining systematic links between the doctrines of creation, conservation and redemption and, on the other, confusing the categories. Moltmann seems to me to come very close to crossing it in this passage.

everything that Jesus of Nazareth is and does is the act of God while not ceasing to be the act of one who is truly human. Jesus is not therefore omniscient and omnipotent; rather, the whole of what he does as incarnate is the work of the omnipotent wisdom of God the Father. There is a communication of actions rather than of attributes.

Before our account is complete, some brief clarification should be attempted of the implications of the doctrine of the divine self-emptying. What is the nature of the suffering that kenosis involves? I have already implied a certain lack of enthusiasm for the concept of the *communicatio idiomatum*. One of its apparent implications, as we have seen, is that if the man Jesus dies on the cross, then we must in some way speak of the death of God. May we say that on the cross God dies? On the whole, I think not. The suggestions it is important to avoid are two. On the one hand, it must not be implied that there is in some sense a rift or opposition within the being of God, as Moltmann's words sometimes imply, with their reference to '*stasis* within God,—"God against God" . . . . We must not allow ourselves to overlook this "enmity" between God and God.'[13] That would be a tritheist denial of the unity of the divine action. On the other hand, there is the corresponding unitarian or monotheist suggestion that one may not here distinguish between the distinctive acts of Father and Son in what Jesus suffers.

The chief requirement here is some measure of clarity on what we believe is happening when Jesus dies on the cross. To see it as primarily or prominently the suffering of God comes dangerously near to reducing atonement to theodicy, and thus using the

---

13. Jürgen Moltmann, *The Crucified God. The Cross of Christ as the Foundation and Criticism of Christian Theology*, translated by R. A. Wilson and John Bowden, London: SCM Press, 1974, pp.

cross chiefly as a means of defending God against responsibility for suffering.[14] This has two unfortunate effects. First, it deprives the death of Jesus of—or at the very least diverts attention away from—its character as truly human action. That is why it should not necessarily be taken as an evasion that the Fathers decided on the qualification, 'one of the three has suffered in the flesh.' It is the office of the Son to suffer. In that, he is indeed doing the work of the Father and doing it in a way that implies that there is a kind of divine suffering involved, in that the Father 'gives up' his Son to death. But if we are not to lose sight of the character of this act as a genuinely human and representative offering of a human life to the Father, we may not centre attention on its being the suffering of God the Father. It is important to remember that the suffering is that undergone by the incarnate Son, the Son fully identified with the order of creation.

Second, to see the suffering of Jesus largely in terms of the suffering of God, is to lose the strong and important biblical teaching that God does not suffer history, he moves it.[15] In that sense, the Father, as the one who sends the Son, is responsible for his death, in the respect that it is in obedience to him that Jesus refuses the last great temptation, to evade the destined outcome of his life of obedience. This does not prevent us seeing the whole incarnation as consequentially the suffering of the whole Godhead. The pattern revealed in the Old Testament is of a divine suffering consequent on the fall, particularly instantiated in the relations of

---

14. For an acute criticism of Moltmann on this score, see Carl E. Braaten, 'A Trinitarian Theology of the Cross', *Journal of Religion* 56 (1976) pp. 113–21. An extended defence of the approach is to be found in Paul Fiddes, *The Creative Suffering of God*, Oxford University Press.

15. The tendency to see history as something suffered by God is of a piece with seeing the origin of the incarnation in evolution: with confusing the world with its lord.

God to Israel. The most concrete expressions of divine suffering in scripture depict it as the result of Israel's covenant infidelity. In terms of our theme, that means that the suffering of God is best seen as the outcome of his relation with the free and fallen creation. In the gospels, that suffering is expressed in the anger of Jesus at sin and evil and his divine sorrow over the moral blindness of Jerusalem (Mt. 23:37f, Lk. 13:34f, 19:41–4). Despite all this, the incarnation and its outcome are primarily to be understood in terms of divine agency rather than divine suffering. It is what must take place if the love of God is actively to overcome the creation's orientation to dissolution. Otherwise, the cross of Jesus will be understood in terms of fate rather than of God's free initiative towards the fallen creation and of a free human response to God's call.

In coming to terms with the mysterious combination of divine determination and human free-will, we cannot escape the paradox: 'this Jesus, delivered up according to the definite plan and foreknowledge of God, you crucified . . .' (Acts 2:23). As has already been affirmed, the whole is the work of the Father, carried out by the Son and Spirit in their distinctive and related ways, and yet the process is at the same time mysteriously advanced by men not fully aware of the significance of their actions. To recapitulate the articulation of all this by the use of the concept of kenosis, we can therefore say that the self-emptying of the eternal Son in the incarnation and passion is an expression of the love of the triune God worked out in the structures of fallen time and space. On the cross, which clearly represents the climax of the kenosis and is its fulfilment, there takes place the plerosis of the Son's self-emptying to our condition which began with the conception of Jesus in the womb of Mary. The Spirit, the agent of the incarnate Son's relation to the Father who sent him, thus brings it about that the shameful death of the incarnate is the means by which the power of God works in and towards the creation.

And that brings us to a link between the burden of the second lecture and the direction of this one. In the second lecture, it was argued that the heart of the work of Christ is to give to the Father the sacrifice of a human life and death perfected through the Spirit's guidance. This lecture enables us to see that it is also to give to the creation the perfection of the eternal love of God. To be God is to be a communion of giving and receiving. The self-giving and receiving that is God take temporal and spatial form in Jesus' kenosis. The Father gives up the Son in the overflow of his love for the world, and receives him back, glorified, through the Spirit. All that happens is fully and wholly the work of the eternal God, while at the same time it is the achievement of a man. The pattern of Philippians 2, it will be remembered, is a pattern of both divine and human self-giving. The self-giving of God and the human life of Jesus correspond to each other because they belong together as two sides of one historic series of events. From conception to death, resurrection and ascension, we have at once God and man, without confusion, without separation, and the rest. Both are to be construed in the language of sacrifice: the Father's giving up of the Son to the horror of life in the fallen world and his consequent death; the Son's giving up of his life to the Father and for that fallen world: both are a kind of sacrifice, a self-giving that actualises in time and space the very life of the Trinity in eternity.

III Kenosis, Creation and Salvation

The concept of sacrifice has been used to denote something of the quality of the divine and human action which is the history of the incarnation. But equally important is the effect of that action—what the sacrificial action of the Son of God achieves and how it achieves it. Briefly, what it achieves is, as we have seen, a reordering of the creation. The incarnation is constitutive of certain worldly realities, it achieves things. The 'how' question is the one that takes us to important new considerations. Simply, the incarnation achieves its redemptive end by a form of divine immanence in the world. The form that immanence takes is what must concern us now. In order to examine the topic we return first to the doctrine of creation, which teaches that everything that is not God has its being only by virtue of the past creation of God, his present conservation, and the directedness towards perfection that they together involve. In that sense, everything that happens is already the result of divine action, so that everything is the action of God. But only in one sense, for the whole point of the doctrine is that the action of God as creator constitutes things as beings in their own right. Here, the crucial relation is a transcendent one: God creates things to be other than himself.

There is, therefore, an absolute distinction to be made between trinitarian theism and pantheism. Divine action as creation is saved from pantheism and necessitarianism by the way in which that action is conceived. Not only is creation through the Son, who is the mediator of God's self-relatedness to that which is not himself, but it is in the Spirit, which means by God's relation to it in otherness. The best illustration of this we have already met. The Holy Spirit represents God's otherness to Jesus: his allowing and enabling him to be himself, free and truly human. He is personally alongside Jesus, present to him as another. He it is who raises from the tomb the body of the crucified Lord and makes him to be eternal mediator between eternity and time. So it is with God's relation to the world. The Spirit sets the creation free to be itself, and so directs it as

God's other to yet find its perfection in the fulfilment of its relation to God. God's power, and that is a concept frequently used of the action of the Spirit, consists in enabling, in directing the creation to perfectedness in freedom.

The stress on otherness is important because it reminds us that the immanence of God can be conceived in such a way as to deprive the creation of its independence and freedom. The more that God is conceived to be identified with the creation, or with parts of it, the more danger there is that it will be deprived of its own most proper being. Pantheism is the extreme form of that denial of otherness. Even the immanence of the Son can be a threat, if it appears to endanger the otherness and freedom of the redeemed. If Christ *is*, without qualification, humankind or even the church, dangerous consequences for human autonomy threaten. An apparent denial of otherness is one reason why some of his critics have accused Barth of bringing God so close that his thought appears deprives the creation of its freedom.

But, the gospel teaches, matters are not quite as simple as that. The situation of the human race is not one of true otherness-in-relation with the creator, but manifests rather a false grasping at otherness which has deprived us of freedom and the creation of its directedness to perfection. In face of the self-inflicted loss of freedom, what is needed is not simply enabling but redemption, and that requires the operation of a form of power over and above that of which we have spoken so far. It requires a new form of immanent divine action through the Son. We have seen what that action is: it is the action of the One through whom all things were made entering the structures of fallen space and time in order to *recreate*—to reorder teleology, to direct again to perfection. And it entails a form of divine immanence. Is then this immanence of the Son a threat to human freedom? That is where we return to the concept of kenosis as a supreme act of power. As kenosis, the condescension of the Son to the human condition is a form of non-coercive yet redemptive and immanent divine action. It is, we might say, not a threatening immanence, as all *general* forms of divine immanence are, but a personal one, and of a particular kind. That is to say, it is a form of immanence—*kenotic* immanence- —which both respects the otherness of the fallen world and reshapes it in a redemptive form of relation to God. If there is truth in Bonhoeffer's famous saying that God allows himself to be driven out of the world on to the cross, it is here. It is misleading if it is asserted in the unqualified way that suggests a form of passivity—for here we have redemptive divine action in the power of the Spirit—but not if treated as a concrete way of conceiving the non-coercive immanence of God in Christ.

To move beyond Bonhoeffer, we must return to the topic of pneumatology which was, it may be remembered, one of the motives for the development of these lectures. The Spirit is God as he empowers the creation to reach its end. As man, Jesus is maintained in truth by the Spirit's direction. As God, he is enabled to take human form in the womb of Mary by virtue of the eschatological action of the Spirit. As mediator between God and man, at once fully God and fully man, he is the channel of that same Spirit who enables the world through him to return to the freedom that is theirs who are children of the Father. The redemptive divine action that is the incarnation of Christ must therefore be understood in terms of power. But it is the power of the Spirit whose function is to perfect creation: that is, to direct the world to its end as creation in saving relation to God. That power has its motor in the self-emptying sacrifice of the Son, which is thus the power of God, but power exerted in a particular non-coercive way. The fourth lecture will be concerned to spell out something of the way in which that redeeming and liberating action takes shape in human action in and towards the world. But before that, some threads must be drawn together.

IV Creation and Redemption

What, in conclusion, are we to say of the relation of creation and redemption? Much has been made already of their close relation. The divine self-emptying is the actualising in time and space of the very love which gives being and form to the world. What, however, is the first of the works of God—first in the sense of prior in intention, if we may so anthropomorphically speak? Here, there are a number of alternative possibilities, which I shall list in somewhat crude form. First, there is the view that redemption is second in the intention of God, because it represents an attempt to make the best of the first, failed, enterprise, that of creation. That rather tendentious way of putting the matter is not fair to some of the more subtle ways of relating creation and redemption, or nature and grace, such as that of Aquinas, whose views can here be taken as representative of the best of that tradition. According to him, the perfection of the creation did not in the first place require Christ. '(F)or the perfection of the universe it is enough for a creature to be ordered in a natural way to God as its goal.' It is, therefore, 'preferable to hold that the work of the incarnation is ordered by God as a remedy for sin, in such a way that if there had been no sin, there would have been no incarnation.'[16] That is to say, the order of the economy of salvation, first creation

---

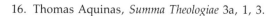

16. Thomas Aquinas, *Summa Theologiae* 3a, 1, 3.

and then redemption, is read back into the eternal purposes of God.

The weakness of such views should be apparent from the direction these lectures have taken from the beginning. Not only do they too easily read from temporal event to divine ordering, but also fail to articulate the initial christological and eschatological thrust of creation. If creation is to an end, namely that all that is should within the structures of time and space come to be perfected in praise of the creator, what we call redemption is not a new end, but the achievement of the original purpose of creation. It only takes the form of redemption—of a 'buying *back*'—because of sin and evil. That does not detract, however, from the basic claim that it is prior. What is realised in the incarnate involvement of the Son in time and space is the redirection of the creation to its original destiny, a destiny that was from the beginning *in Christ*, for all creation is through and to the Son.

 Such a point brings us to the second way of structuring the relation of creation and redemption, and it is that of Karl Barth. As is well known, Barth makes what is fundamentally the right choice: the covenant is the inner basis of creation, creation the external basis of the covenant. The creation becomes the realm on which the glorious covenant love of God shall take shape: the *theatrum gloriae dei*. Unfortunately, there are flaws in Barth's formulation which, in what is now something like a critical consensus, make creation not only second to covenant, but subordinate in a way that detracts from the fullness of the order of creation. The problem is to be found in the way Barth expounds the concept of covenant in terms of election. Election, that 'in Himself, in the primal and basic decision in which He wills to be and actually is God . . . . God is none other than the One who in His Son or Word elects Himself and in and with Himself elects His people' is at the centre of things.[17] Because in his inner being God is an electing God, both creation and redemption are embraced within the concept of election, and so brought into a coherent relation with one another which ensures a fundamental weighting to redemption.

Without doubt, the value of this shift from the old Calvinist or, more accurately, Augustinian conception of election is immense. No longer is the fundamental eschatological directedness of human life conceived dualistically towards both heaven and hell as equal possibilities—or even tilting hellwards—but the will of God is generously conceived as intending universal redemption. But, as has often been pointed out, an eternal and thus pretemporal election, generous or no, tends to order all things to a beginning not of the kind suggested in these lectures, but to one whose character is rather at the expense of an eschatological directedness. Everything important seems already to have happened. Barth's is a strongly immanentist theology —christologically immanent—in which the kenotic dimensions tend to lose their power. Similarly, real eschatology is lost, or at least suggests only the playing out of that which has already been decided in advance in a way that endangers the freedom at once of the Spirit and of the creation. It is noteworthy that in Barth election is conceived rather binitarianly: as something happening between Father and Son. The Spirit contributes nothing structurally, as in much of Barth's theology. And there is another equally problematic feature: election appears to be oriented almost wholly to the human species, to the relative neglect of the outer basis, the creation as a whole.[18]

17. Karl Barth, *Church Dogmatics*, II/2, 1957, p. 76. As the following remarks will show, I now withdraw much of my criticism of David Ford's interpretation of Barth, made in 'Review Article: Barth and God's Story', *Scottish Journal of Theology* 37 (1984) pp. 373–380.

18. See Andrew Linzey *The Neglected Creature*, PhD University of London, 1986.

Therefore we must attempt a third way of relating creation and redemption, whose centre is still Jesus Christ but whose working out is more shaped by pneumatological concerns. What is the end of creation? That all things may through being perfected praise the one who made them.[19] The love of the Father is given outward form in the free and unnecessitated creation of a world whose dynamically oriented form is that it should come to be perfected through time and in space in praise of its maker. The human race is given on earth the task of realising this perfectedness, through our relation to God, through our relation with each other, and through our care of the non-personal creation, which cannot be perfected without us. It is clear that such a divine purpose is prior to, and yet encompasses within itself, a fall which would unaccountably—and we can find no reason for evil—impede the creation's completion. We can therefore agree with those who have argued that, had there been no fall, it would have still have been the Father's good pleasure to come into personal relation with us through the incarnation of his Son. (That is often called the Scotist view of the incarnation.)[20] We can also speculate that such an incarnation would not have taken the form that it did, for, as Irving rightly held, the formal or immediate cause of the way that things took shape is the sin of the creature, even though the first cause is the eternal will of God for fellowship with the creature.[21]

---

19. When he was listening to Mozart, Barth saw this truth that his concentration on election otherwise made difficult for him. See *Church Dogmatic* III/3, 1960, pp. 298f.

20. See Brian L. Horne, *A World to Gain. Incarnation and the Hope of Renewal*, London: Darton, Longman and Todd, 1983.

21. Edward Irving, *The Collected Writings of Edward Irving*, edited by G. Carlyle, London: Alexander Strahan, 1865, volume V, p. 10.

Once again, Irenaeus can be taken as something of a model, because he understands together both the material context of salvation and the eschatological orientation of creation. The tendency of Augustinian thought is to treat creation merely or largely in terms of beginnings. Now, without doubt, the notion of an absolute beginning to space and time is essential to Christian theology. Without it, we lose the finitude, contingency and otherness from God which are so important for an understanding of the limited but real autonomy of the created order. But if that beginning is all that is stressed in the doctrine of creation, the teleological dynamic that Irenaeus has learned from the New Testament is lost. Creation is not merely through Christ, but *to* him: from the beginning, it has an eschatological thrust. Salvation takes place *within* the created and material order with an eye to the perfection of that which was begun.

Jesus Christ is the one through whom all things take their shape and to whom the Spirit directs them. When the Spirit shapes him a body from the flesh of Mary, what we see is not just the working out of election—though we do see that—but the renewing of the whole of creation, the redirecting of the world to its end. Only through his cross is the creation 'redeemed from its fault and shame' so that it may be perfected in praise of its creator and redeemer. Some such account, it seems to me, can take into itself the strengths of Barth's placing of the covenant in the very heart of God without the danger of appearing to incorporate every-thing into Christ in advance, and without the tendency to an anthropocentric exclusion of the non-human creation from the process. The teleology of the whole creation, past, present and and to come is shaped through Christ: begun through him, reordered to its end through his self-emptying, and directed to him as its end. On a conception such as this, the enabling of creation's praise of the creator becomes a central part of the human offering of thanks to God for his creating and redeeming love.[22] Something of how that takes form in our time will be my concern in the final lecture.

22. Jeremy Begbie, *Voicing Creation's Praise. Towards a Theology of the Arts*, Edinburgh: T & T Clark, 1991.

In the Image and Likeness of God

I The Nature of the Image

In the first chapter of Genesis come the words: 'And God created man in his own image; male and female created he them.' There are two chief ways in which the passage is generally used to form theological anthropology today. The first is to concentrate on the 'male and female', and to say, after Barth, that our imaging consists in the fact that we are male and female in relationship.[1] There is much to be said for the view, but other stages of argument are required before the place of the male–female polarity—what kind of imaging there is—can be adequately treated. The second concentrates on the broader context in which talk of imaging appears: the giving of the earth into the dominion of the human race. There is much to be said for this view too. Not only does it fit the immediately following command, but it makes sense of much that is said in the following two chapters of the relation of

1. Karl Barth, *Church Dogmatics*, translation edited by G. W. Bromiley and T. F. Torrance, volume III/2, Edinburgh: T & T Clark, 1958, pp. 183ff.

Adam and Eve to the earth-garden they are to tend.
Here, too, however, there are intermediate steps to be
taken. They are christological and trinitarian.

It has not escaped the notice of commentators on
the doctrine of the image of God that in the New
Testament the meanings of both of the words used in
Genesis, 'image' and 'likeness' are reordered to Christ.
With one or two exceptions, the old doctrine in its
purely anthropological form has disappeared in favour
of the teaching that Christ is the image of God. He is not
only the true image of God, but also the source of
human renewal in it. 'He is the image of the invisible
God' (Col. 1:15); 'predestined to be conformed to the
image of his Son' (Rom. 8:29). What does this mean?
First, that Jesus represents God to the creation in the
way that the first human beings were called, but failed,
to do; and second that he enables other human beings
to achieve the directedness to God of which their
fallenness has deprived them. If we look back to the
first lecture, we shall recall that a large part of Jesus'
ministry was concerned with the redemption into
obedience to God of the fallen created order. As such,
his activity was the exercise of the true image and
likeness of God. From the second lecture, we learn that
as the representative human being he offers to the
Father the first-fruits of the redeemed creation, the free
obedience that consists in a sacrifice of both soul and
body to its maker. This led us to a concept of mediation.
As the ascended Lord, the risen Christ opens up earth
to heaven and heaven to earth. It is worth observing
that it is of the risen and ascended Christ that many of
the passages ascribing the image to him refer. Colossians 1:15 could again be cited, as could the third verse
of that meditation on the ascension, the Letter to the
Hebrews. From the third lecture we learn something
more of the nature of the mediation: that Christ is not
only a representative human being, but, as the one born

before the foundation of the world, he images the Father in a unique way.

I have also suggested that the whole structure can best be understood in a trinitarian framework. Christ the incarnate, crucified, risen and ascended Son comes from the Father through the Spirit and in due time gives that same Spirit as the way by which the creation may through him return to the Father. Imaging is therefore a triune act: the Son images the Father as through the Spirit he realises a particular pattern of life on earth. By thus transposing the development into the language of image, we find that a dynamic emerges. The representative bearer of the image becomes, as the channel of the Spirit, the vehicle of the renewal of the image in those who enter into relation with him. There is a 'change into his likeness' (2 Cor. 3:18), a 'being renewed in knowledge after the image of the creator' (Col. 3:10).

Let us look back, through the focus provided by the conception of imaging as a triune act, to the Old Testament passages with which we began. There were, as we saw, two dimensions: being male and female and being given dominion over the creation. If, first, to be created in the image of God is to be made male and female, what is implied is that in this most central of all human relatedness is to be found a finite echo of the relatedness of Father, Son and Holy Spirit. To be God, according to the doctrine of the Trinity, is to be persons in relation: to be God only as a communion of being. It is that which is replicated, at the finite level, by the polarity of male and female: to be in the image of God is to be called to a relatedness-in-otherness that echoes the eternal relatedness-in-otherness of Father, Son and Spirit. This is not to say that we may read what is now called gender back into the deity: rather, simply, that human beings are called to a life in relation that is most truly instantiated in the polarity of male and female.

The second dimension of our imagedness suggested by Genesis is in the area of our dominion over the creation. The human calling, as made concrete in the incarnation of the mediator, is, simply put, to enable the creation to praise its maker. The Western Christian tradition has not for the most part succeeded in giving adequate account of this dimension of things, and has put too many of its eggs in the basket of individual and, more recently, social and political redemption, at the expense of the wider material context. That is why Christian theology is particularly weak in its treatment of two areas of human action: art and what can to be called ecological ethics. If we are to restore a proper emphasis in these two areas, we must find a renewed theology of the image of God.

We can begin by saying that to be in the image of God is to be placed in a dynamic of relationships: first of all with other human beings and second with the rest of the created order. This ordering to the personal and non-personal world is, to use the spatial imagery of previous lectures, to be understood first in terms of vertical relationships. The dynamic of the image derives from our relationship with God the creator and redeemer, so that to be created is to be oriented, in the time and space he has given, to a perfection of being for and in him. To be in the image of God is not, therefore, to have some timeless quality like reason, or anything else, but to exist in a directedness, between our coming from nothing and our being brought through Christ before the throne of the Father. That teleology or directedness places us, second, in a certain situation, different for each particular human being, in that network of relationships we have called horizontal, so that what we have called the image of God works itself out—or fails to work itself out—first in relations with other human beings and second in a relatedness of responsibility for the non-personal creation. *To be in the image of God is therefore to be called to represent God to the* creation and the creation to God, so enabling it to reach its perfection.

But, as we have seen, such an imaging forth can be achieved only as the result of a re-ordering. Because the image is distorted by sin, its true dynamic is realised only through redemption, as the Spirit conforms us to Christ, the crucified and ascended Lord. There is, accordingly, a double focus: first on the cleansing of the image, and second on the completion of that which was begun. We are concerned at once with renewal and perfection, or rather with perfection through renewal. Our first task, then is to say something of the notion of the image as distorted or defaced, and in need of cleansing and reorientation.

II The Distortion of the Image

If there is a fallenness of the human race and, along with it, of the world—as we have seen that the relations of Christ and creation require us to hold—it is scarcely surprising that it should take its most destructive toll in the two areas we have outlined, inter-personal relations, and particularly human sexuality, and our relations with the rest of the creation. It can be, and frequently is argued that past generations of Christians have stressed too much the link between sexuality and sin, too little the social and political determinants of human alienation. In so far as such treatment has derived from a generally negative assessment of human sexuality, the current change of emphasis to the social shape of sin would seem to be justified. And yet it can be argued that there is now a danger of over-reaction. If our being made as male and female is at the centre of the way in which we are called to be in the image of God, it may well follow that it is in our sexual relationships—sexual in the broader sense of relations

in general between men and women, not only hus-
bands and wives but parents and children, employer
and employee, teacher and taught—that will be found
the greater opportunities for both good and ill.

The negative side, more than apparent in our
society, is that at least as much damage and unhappi-
ness, activity that makes for death rather than for life, is
to be found in human sexual relations than in economic
oppression, political tyranny and ecological disaster.
This is because the closer our relatedness to another
person, the greater potential there is for both good and
ill radiating thence to the wider world. It is where we
come most directly into relationship with other people
that what we are as persons, and therefore our relations
with everyone and everything else, take their essential
shape. We are, in our day, more aware of the damage
that is caused by virtue of the disorder in our relations
with the non-personal world. Quite enough is written
about that already, so that my chief concern is to ask:
what is there in common between the two forms of
alienation I have sketched—person to person and
person to world—that enables us to develop our theme
of the relation between our being in the image of God
and the teaching that the true image is to be found in
Jesus Christ?

In both cases it can be suggested that idolatry, in
the sense of giving to anything created the value of
God, is the essential cause of the misdirectedness, the
directedness of the creation to dissolution, that I have
suggested is the heart of the defacing of the image. It is
here that we must refer to Paul's analysis of the human
fall in terms of idolatry in the first chapter of the Letter
to the Romans. It is instructive that the first fruits of
idolatry are to be found in disorderly sexual relationships, and that the disorder is held to stem directly from
worshipping the creature rather than the creator (v. 25).
From a distorted relation to God stem the distorted

interpersonal relations which wreak such havoc with the dynamic of the image of God.

Similarly, that the ecological crisis results from the worship of that which is not God is easier to establish, if only because such an interpretation is more fashionable. I shall, therefore, simply indicate the heart of the matter, and make two points. The first is that all human dominion of the earth will involve the alteration of the balance of things, and that no human behaviour, however well-intentioned, will be free from problematic consequences. There is therefore no natural cure, no solution to be read off nature, of the problems caused by human relatedness with the rest of the created order, so that there will always be an ecological problem. (The theological significance of this will be touched on later.) The second is that such problems as there are are compounded by human fallenness and its tendency to pollute whatever it touches. To understand that fallenness as the result of idolatry, is to call attention to the human tendency to displace God as the centre of the universe as the heart of the problem.

The failure of relation to God is therefore the root of both personal and ecological orientation. It is a feature of all eras of history, but can be seen in the Enlightenment and its current aftermath in its most glaring colours. Human self-divinization is to be seen in the sometimes conscious attempt to transfer to man the attributes of divinity: omniscience, omnipotence, etc., and in the corresponding treatment of the world as a mere object to which we may behave as we wish. The classic illustration is to be found in Descartes' theory that animals were merely machines. 'Descartes's explicit aim had been to make men "lords and possessors of nature". It fitted in well with his intention that he should have portrayed other species as inert and lacking any spiritual dimension. In so doing, he created an absolute break between man and the rest of nature, thus clearing the way very satisfactorily for the uninhibited exercise of human rule.'[2] Here we come close to the flaws in the deepseated Christian tradition of seeing the image of God to consist in reason, which cannot be absolved of some of the blame for the way things have developed. Reason is so easily conceived as the source of control, absolute or otherwise. In this respect, the teachings of the Enlightenment appear to be the result of taking to their logical limit tendencies already present within the Christian tradition. But the general point that is being illustrated from that era of European history is that what can rather barbarously be called the mechanisation or technologisation of reality is a fruit of the idolatrous worship of human capacity; and that is the form in which the ecological problem meets us today.

III *The Re-forming of the Image in Christ and the Church*

If sin and fallenness derive from that distortion of relatedness to God that takes shape in idolatry, it follows that the work of Christ in realisation and restoration of the divine image consists in the enabling of non-idolatrous forms of human being in the world. Here, once again, the themes of the second lecture come to the fore. There we learned that the heart of the human work of Christ was, through the Spirit, to offer to the Father the wholeness of a human life. In him is to be seen the first fruits of a human life that has been freed from the pollution disseminated in the world by its misuse for other purposes than the praise of God. Thus is the creation, closed off from God by sin, opened

2. Keith Thomas, *Man and the Natural World. Changing Attitudes in England 1500–1800*, London: Penguin Books, 1984, pp. 34f.

up to the Father. The link between his imaging and ours is derived from the focus of the third lecture, that the self-emptied Son, and so the Son fulfilled in self-giving for others, is, as ascended to the side of the Father, the mediator of the same Spirit that enabled his free self-offering. Thus is God's self-opening to the creation in the incarnation of his Son made a way for the redemption of all flesh. That the image of God is centred on Christ means therefore not only that he is the pattern for our approach to the world, but that the creation can be truly itself only by being conformed to him through the Spirit.

What, then, is the outcome of the gift of the Spirit through the ascended Christ? In a word, freedom: freedom from the idolatry of self and the world, and freedom for patterns of relatedness that are towards life and not death. But the question now is: what form must freedom take in a fallen world? How does redemption work itself out in a world that would go to dissolution rather than be perfected before its creator? The question can be rephrased: how is the divine image reformed in those in whom it has been distorted out of all recognition? In passing, it is worth remarking that one advantage of this way of looking at the question is that it frees us from engagement in futile disputes about whether or not the image of God is lost at the fall. The most futile of all discussions in recent times relates the question of the image to that of natural theology. Have we or have we not so lost the image that we may have knowledge of God apart from revelation? This seems to me a false question above all because it treats the question of the image in terms of rationality. If we ask, in a different way, whether the image of God is still exercised after the Fall, we can say: yes, in so far as there is unadulterated love between man and woman, in so far as there are genuine forms of human community, and in so far as the creation is allowed in industry, agriculture, art and craft to praise its maker and to be directed to its perfection in him. But we must also say: no, in the sense that this side of the end there is no human love unadulterated by selfishness and misplaced lust, and no human action towards the world not in some way polluted by greed, exploitation and a grasping for divinity. The re-formation of the image is thus to be conceived as freedom in a double sense: as freedom *from* idolatry and freedom *for* redeemed relationships with person and world. But how does such reshaping take place? The answer to that question is that it takes place in worship and life, not, of course, as two completely separate forms of being in the world, but as two sides of the same dynamic.

It is for reasons such as this that we must locate the beginning of the re-formation of the image of God in the church, not because the church is immune from contamination by the network of dissolution, but because the church is the community placed by Word and sacrament under the rule of Christ and therefore in saving relation to God the creator and redeemer. It is, to adapt Calvin's famous words, the place where Christ is present so long as the word is truly preached and the sacraments duly administered. As such, and only as such, the Church becomes the locus of the human freedom that is the gift of the Lord who is the Spirit, for where there are the Word and sacraments, there is the change 'into his likeness.' Notice here the connection of ideas in 2 Cor 3:17f: 'where the Spirit of the Lord is, there is freedom. And we all . . . are being changed into his likeness . . . . For this comes from the Lord who is the Spirit.'

In order, however, to avoid falling into the traps of idealising the church or of treating it apart from the action of God, a number of connections must be made which have been rather inadequately treated in the tradition. It is not much of a caricature to say that the church has often been regarded as the place where what is essentially a private and inward experience may be developed and nurtured. Even Calvin falls into this trap, treating the church as one of 'the external means . . . by which God invited us into the society of Christ and holds us therein.'[3] Newman is even worse. As one commentator has said, 'The Church . . . is for Newman a collection of individual atoms held together . . . by an essentially *political* bond. The Church is an "imperial" power exercising over its members "an absolute and almost despotic rule".'[4] To put it in the terms used in these lectures, we can say that according to such a theology, the church appears to be that part of the created order which happens, merely contingently, to be used as a focus or vehicle of salvation for otherwise unrelated individuals. Yet we must not, in awareness of the triumphalist ideologies of the church that have often stained Christian history, in reaction claim too little for the action of God within the created order that the church represents. If this is the means that God has chosen, and the biblical evidence for such a view is overwhelming, then we are faced not with a *mere* but rather with a *saving* contingency, like that of the humanity of Jesus Christ. What God contingently chooses becomes the means of the redemption of the order of creation.

Here we reach a crucial stage of the argument. It is important to draw links between a theology of the incarnate image of God in Christ, as it was set out in the previous lectures, and the church if the pitfalls to the left and to the right are to be avoided; that is, if we are neither to despise the empirical church nor to make it falsely absolute. We have seen that Christ's (empirical)

---

3. John Calvin, *Institutes of the Christian Religion*, from the title of Book IV.
4. David Nicholls, *The Independent*, 27th October 1990.

humanity derived at once from the Father's will to redemption and the Spirit's work in enabling a true human life to take shape in the incarnate. That latter point makes an essential link possible. It is the Holy Spirit's act to *make particular*, and it is in the notion of particularity that we find the link we are seeking. We often think of the Spirit as the one who makes universal the work of Christ. But, if he does, it is by realising in time *particular* instantiations of the perfection that belongs to eternity. In Jesus' case, the Spirit establishes his particular humanity as the Jewish man who was the true messiah of Israel. The church is by analogy—and only by analogy, for the church is not Christ—to be seen as the object of the Spirit's particularizing of the action of the ascended Christ in the world. It is there that is to be found the link between Jesus' being in the image of God and human being in it in conformity to him—in its being shaped to him.

According to one well-known and much used expression in Paul, the form that the Spirit's particularizing action takes is a being of people 'in Christ', in the community that is his body. It is noteworthy how often that community is claimed to be the place of the reshaping of human relationships, specifically in Gal. 3:28 including that between man and woman. (Surely those commentators are right who hold that to say there is 'no male or female' in Christ is not to abolish the differences of sex, but to reconcile them.) The church is thus the community where fallen forms of relationship are invalidated and outgrown: are unlearned through the grace of God and the work of the Spirit. It is important to remember that what is involved is not instant transformation, but a reordering of teleology or directedness.

There are two features of ecclesiology, therefore, which obviate a triumphalist understanding: the free and unpredictable action of the Spirit and its eschatological orientation. The stress on the freedom of the Spirit is important, because it is partly the result of an inadequately pneumatological understanding of the church that aspects of her life have been so subject to distortion. Claims to be able automatically to channel the Spirit, through an order of clergy, for example, have led to a false institutionalizing of the Church, while on the other hand the making of the church simply the outer vehicle of an inner experience have claimed too little for the reshaping of social relations which can be expected in a community which is the body of Christ. Rather, a true theology of the church will see it as the place—institution, even—where human life experiences not instant perfection but a new directedness towards community: that is, toward the community of the last days which is relationship with the triune God and through that with the other who is the neighbour. The one—Godwards—movement is the source and teleology of the second. And it is in the Spirit as the one through whom the end is realised that the movement in both directions can be understood to take shape. By relating to God through Christ, the Spirit redirects human energies and actions in the world.

In the case of Jesus, as we saw, his imaging of God was realised in the offering to the Father, through the Spirit, of a particular form of relatedness to other human beings and the creation. The resurrection made universal and so representative the form of life, the human teleology, that Jesus was and is. The church accordingly, must be understood as the community where that representative humanity becomes the form of the teleology of others. That is one reason why worship, as the conscious ordering of a form of human activity to God through the Son set forth in both word and sacrament is so important. It is not, of course, the primary motive for worship, which is a human turning to God simply for himself. Insofar, however, as we are considering here the matter of the forming of the image of God—the impact of the risen and ascended Christ upon forms of human being—it will necessarily come into prominence. The image of God takes shape, is renewed, as human beings are formed in community by the Spirit through Christ. (It is as a reflex, so to speak, of this process of being conformed to Christ that the church's wider social and political responsibilities should be understood).

In considering the personal and social shaping of the image we should not be hesitant in reaffirming the Reformation emphasis on the place of human words in the shaping of our imaging of God. It must be emphasised not only that words are part of the creation—that they often appear to be 'mere words' is a feature of human fallenness—and that the gospel presentations of Jesus show him as achieving the redemption of the created order largely through what he says. When the prophets of Israel speak the word given them by God, things happen simply by virtue of those words being spoken. Nor should we be so concerned to counter a false emphasis on the centring of the image of God in reason that we forget that for Paul redemption, the ability to offer to God our bodies as a living sacrifice, takes form through the renewing of the mind (Rom. 12:1f). Similarly, the danger of much recent theology, especially that forming the life of the churches today, is that it will be so dominated by activism—with churches doing things, changing the world, achieving justice, etc.—that we shall forget that at the centre of both Old and New Testament concerns is the matter of teaching. The first source of the renewal of the image, the reshaping of human directedness, is a sitting under the word which is the representation, actualising indeed, of the story of the Word incarnate; in the words of Colossians, 'being renewed *in knowledge* after the image of the creator' (Col. 3:10).

It is only after we have established that centre that we may turn to the sacraments which are on the face of things more obviously concerned with relating Christ and creation in the life of the church. Without wanting to downgrade the sacraments, which are essential ways of expressing the incarnation of the Son and the consequent involvement of the church in the life of the whole world, we must reaffirm the tradition of both Augustine and the Reformers that there is no sacrament without word, without some word of divine promise that the material creation is able to be the vehicle of divine action in and towards the world. This is important for a number of reasons, but among them, I would like to suggest, is the due ordering of the relation of persons and world. The Friend of the Earth, Jonathan Porritt, was recently reported as saying that a tree is as important as a human person. If that is so, the response must be that that way lies fanaticism and tyranny—and, indeed, that very idolatry which is the source of our loss of the image of God. As I suggested at the end of the first lecture, the world of trees is not destined for a salvation of its own, even though it has its due part to play in the redemption of all things. Water, bread and wine are vehicles of a personal relationship and not of cosmic process. They represent the fact that the eternal Son of God took our flesh in order to make it was it was created to be.

Following Genesis we can then say that the human imaging of God takes shape in two forms of horizontal relatedness: with other people and with the rest of the created world. The restoration of the image in the life of the church repeats that double reorientation, but in a definite order. Relations of human beings with the world are restored in a body whose prior ethical calling is the creation of a community of persons. Human fallenness is chiefly revealed in breaches of community: between man and woman, but also between human beings in all the personal and social institutions without which we are not truly ourselves. So far as their ethical—horizontal—dimension—which, of course derives from the vertical relationality we have been concerned to expound—is concerned, the sacraments of baptism and the Lord's Supper before all else operate to shape a particular pattern of community in the form of Christ. They are the way the sacrifice of Christ takes form in the world. That is why, whatever disagreements there may be about the detailed exegesis of I Corinthians 11, it is quite clear that the relation between what we might call an invalid liturgical celebration and breaches of human communion is at the very centre of Paul's offence with the behaviour of the church. Offences against community are what invalidate the eucharist, not the person of the president or the uttering of the wrong words. One reason is that sacraments are what they are by virtue of their enabling of human belonging in the church. That is one reason why it is wrong to call marriage a sacrament. One can be truly married, and 'in the sight of God', without stepping inside a church. Baptism and the Lord's Supper, by contrast, are what they are as sacraments of, respectively, entry into a community formed around the sacrifice of Christ and the maintenance of the community without which the church would not be the embodiment of the image of God.

According to such an understanding of the sacraments, the material elements become the means of the formation of human community. The water of baptism is to be understood, in this respect, as the way in which the kenosis of the Son of God, his self-giving to death, is made the pattern of life for the one entering the community that represents the incarnate one on earth. It is a patterning in two senses, as is often pointed out. The symbol of washing represents a cleansing from pollution while the symbol of dying a giving up of the worship of the self that is the ultimate outcome and form of idolatry. The Lord's Supper, the sacrament of continuing membership of the body of Christ, shifts the emphasis from the judgement of the old form of life—though that is still there (1 Cor. 11:31f)—to the eschatological theme of transformation. That is why it is often linked to the idea of the heavenly banquet. Meals are in almost universal human experience linked with notions of celebration and of community. Food is best eaten in company, and so the Lord's Supper becomes the means by which the praise of God and the transformation of human life out of alienation and into the eschatological community are at once symbolised and realised.

The primary dynamic of the material elements is, as we have seen, in relation to human community. But that is no reason why we should not also find in them relevance for human use of the world in general. Because the created world is used in the praise of God here, it may rightly be used in the praise of God in other contexts, too. Just as the Holy Spirit makes the sacramental elements into the vehicles at once of the praise of God and of the creation of human community, so the human calling is to enable through that same Spirit all the creation to praise its maker. That calling or enabling is, like the sacraments, eschatological in its orientation. Creation, as we have seen, has an end: that all things may be offered, perfected and transformed, to their creator. The primary offering, just like the primary realisation of human community, is made in worship. It follows that unless there takes place a renewal of human relatedness to God, there will be neither true community nor redemption and perfection of the creation. That is why, to return to the statement made at the beginning of the section, the church is the place where we must locate our first account of the re-forming of the image of God. The image is re-formed and so realised in the process of human conformation to Christ by the action of the eschatological Spirit.

IV The Dynamic of the Image in the World

One central way in which the human imaging of God can be articulated is through an ethic of sacrifice. I am fully aware of the dangers of using that word, for it can be, and often has, been used as a means of imposing an ethic of submission on others. The point has nowhere been better put than by Donald MacKinnon in his essay in *Objections to Christian Belief*:

> (T)he idiom of sacrifice is . . . deadly in the ideas and attitudes which it encourages . . . To sacrifice ourselves is, it is said, to realize the image of the crucified, whereas the self-sacrificing may simply be mutilating himself, purposively destroying the sweetness of existence in the name of illusion, in order to make himself a hero in his own eyes.[5]

As the examples used by MacKinnon in the development of his theme show, the objection has much to do with the moral objectionableness of using a concept as a lever in a process of religious blackmail. It would, however, to put it mildly, be a strange Christian ethic that did not allow for the possibility that being conformed to the image of Christ may involve the

---

5. Donald MacKinnon, 'Moral Objections', *Objections to Christian Belief*, London: Constable, 1963, pp. 23f. Other valuable accounts of the misuse of the concept of sacrifice are to be found in the papers by Sheridan Gilley and Ann Loades in *Sacrifice and Redemption. Durham Essays in Theology*, edited by S. W. Sykes, Cambridge University Press, 1991, pp. 218–234 and 247–261.

giving up, on the analogy of the cross, of something \
important, even life. A crucial requirement, however, is
to embrace such concerns within the kind of theology of
sacrifice that has been outlined throughout the lectures.
The emphasis here is not on giving up, absolutely and
without qualification, but on offering to God that
creation which he has placed in our hands. Under the
conditions of fallenness, that may sometimes involve
sacrifices in the old sense, of the kind whose debased
version so roused the objections of Donald MacKinnon,
but should certainly not involve the imposing upon
others of life-denying patterns of behaviour. The heart
of the matter is quite the reverse.

A more adequate ethic of sacrifice will involve a
double orientation: to what we do with our persons,
with ourselves as souls and bodies, and to what we do
with the rest of the world. An expansion of the first
orientation will consist in large part of an exegesis of
Romans 12:1: 'present your bodies as a living sacrifice,
holy and acceptable to God, which is your spiritual
worship.' The RSV translation is a bad one, though the
use of the word 'living' should be noted, especially in
view of MacKinnon's strictures. The Greek word
translated 'spiritual' is in fact 'logical', and can mean
just that. The logic of our embodiedness, of our
createdness in the image of God, is the presentation of a
certain shape of being before the throne of God. Such
logic will concern in large part our relatedness to other
people, for there is no action, however apparently
private, that does not have implications for our life with
others. In articulating what it means, the notion of
sacrifice with which we have been working will operate
as a criterion: if an act or form of relatedness with
ourselves or with other people can be rightly offered to
God as the praise of his creation, then it is appropriately
called an exercise of the image of God.

The same kind of criterion operates in our consideration of the second aspect of our being in the image of God, our exercise of dominion over the creation. I shall give more attention to this side of the matter, because of the concentration of the lectures on Christ and creation. I believe, however, that these relationships are in general of less importance for our humanity than those called personal, for reasons which should by now be apparent. I also believe that we are as a culture and civilisation as confused and disordered about personal relationships as we are about our use of the creation, and that the current preoccupation with things ecological may be obscuring this. In many matters, such as those concerning the rights and wrongs of the practice of abortion, it is clear that the two questions, of what we do with our bodies and what we do with the world, are very close indeed, and cannot be treated in isolation from one another. However, in order to expound the chief implications of the doctrine of the image of God, I shall treat here a somewhat less complicated topic.

The question of the use we make of the creation brings into focus one of the oddest features of our modern world, its divorce of the worlds of work and of art, of function and of beauty. We live in a world where the pursuit of work is for the most part conceived in economic terms and the world of aesthetics treated quite separately, often in terms of high culture or recreation ('leisure'). That is in general, it seems to me, a form of fragmentation of human experience that replicates the structures of fallenness rather than those of the teleology of creation. It is not surprising that modern Western culture shows so many of the signs of fragmentation. It is certainly not within the power of churches and theologians to offer instant cures for the ills of modernity, which are after all not in quality different from those of all civilizations. What we can and should offer is a vision of what it is to be in the image of God and a consideration of how we should seek to embody it in our communities of worship and life.

We can approach the question of the ethic of sacrifice through an examination of the human priesthood of creation. (Indeed, to prevent misunderstanding, perhaps we would be better to speak all along of an ethic of priesthood.) To be in the image of God, it can be argued, is to be called to exercise our *dominium terrae* as those who are priests. As the priest offers the animal without blemish on the altar, so we are to offer all the creation with which we have to do—all that is bound up most closely with us in the network of created reality —to God the Father. This is not, of course, an independent or autonomous ethic. It takes shape only as we are conformed to the image of the Son and as the Spirit enables, through him, anticipations to take place of the promised perfection of all things. Yet since it is truly human work, as human as that achieved by Jesus through the Spirit, it can be considered in relative independence, assuming in the background the things that have already been said of the pneumatological dimension of true human action.

The human priesthood of the creation first came to modern expression through its use in connection with science. The most recent exponent of the notion is Professor T. F. Torrance. Interpreting the thought of Francis Bacon, he writes:

> Science is a religious duty, while man as scientist can be spoken of as *the priest of creation*, whose task it is to interpret the books of nature, to understand the universe in its wonderful structures and harmonies, and to bring it all into orderly articulation, so that it fills its proper end as the vast theatre of glory in which the Creator is worshipped and praised. Nature itself is dumb, but it is man's part to bring it to word, to be its mouth through

which the whole universe gives voice to the glory and majesty of the living God.[6]

In contrast to and to some extent against Torrance is the view of John Zizioulas, which is that there should be a broader, more generally ecologically oriented concept of human priesthood. His criticism of Torrance is that his conception construes our relation to creation too much in terms of knowledge and rationality. (To that extent, it might appear to be too much in the tradition of conceiving the image of God in terms of reason.) Whether that is entirely fair to Torrance's position, there can be little doubt that particularly insofar as knowledge is linked primarily with control, as it is in some modern philosophy of science, certain conceptions of science can be seen to be essentially alienating, and so to be at or near the root of the ecological problem. The introduction of the idea of priesthood undoubtedly mitigates the problems of the approach. To place any activity in relation to God is to put it into some proportion, and so to avoid the extremes of human self-deification—for example, those inherent in 'technocracy'—which are even nearer to the root of the ecological problem. Ironically, Zizioulas' own position can lead to the same tendency of over-stressing human activity towards the world, while under-rating a listening to and response to the God-given structures of createdness.

At the heart of Zizioulas' approach is an ethic of creativity: '(In) being the Priest of creation man is also a creator, and, perhaps, we may say that in all of his truly creative activities there is hidden a para-priestly character.'[7] The theological problem with this conception is

6. Thomas F. Torrance, *Transformation and Convergence in the Frame of Knowledge. Explorations in the Interrelations of Scientific and Theological Enterprise*, Belfast: Christian Journals, 1984, pp. 263f.

7. John D. Zizioulas, 'Preserving God's Creation. Three Lectures on Theology and Ecology. III,' *King's Theological Review* 13 (1990) p. 5.

that it makes our imaging of God to consist not in certain forms of relatedness to others and the world, but in what is not a defining characteristic of God, creativity. God is, indeed, our creator, so that we can say that the act of creation is not foreign to the way that he is as Father, Son and Spirit. But it is of the essence of God's freedom-in-relatedness that he is not bound to create. He would still be God if he had not created this world or any other. The distinction between the immanent and economic trinities implied in such an affirmation is important because it enables it to be said that although creation is indeed the work of God, yet because it is the *free* work of God the world is by it enabled to be authentically itself. While, therefore, we are indeed creative beings—although with J. R. R. Tolkien I prefer to talk of our sub-creation, on the grounds that only God is truly creator—it is not creativity in which our imaging of God consists.

The point of all this is that the stress must be not on *our*, subjectively conceived, activity, whether of knowledge, dominance, control or creativity, so much as on the way in which the creation is by our action enabled to be itself. As debates about the use of Antarctica and of some areas of wilderness indicate, the ends of creation may best sometimes be served by human *in*activity. But where we are concerned with human action, it is in this context that we can treat the ways in which we may link the worlds of work and play, of function and art. To image the being of God towards the world, to be the priest of creation, is to behave towards the world in all its aspects, of work and of play, in such a way that it may come to be what it was created to be, that which praises its maker by becoming perfect in its own way. In all this, there is room for both usefulness and beauty to take due place, but differently according to differences of activity and object. We do not expect a bootscraper to be of the same beauty as a

Constable landscape, or the latter to be as functional as the former. Yet if the former is of rank ugliness, its usefulness will be sullied, while if the latter is kept in the vault of a bank it will not perform the function for which it is designed. Different products of the human mind and hand are differently related to us and to the rest of the world, and yet can be understood equally to need to be shaped in ways to which the categories of both beauty and usefulness can in different ways be applied—for everything is what it is and not another thing. Science can certainly be understood in this respect as one of the jewels in the crown of the human priesthood.

Once again, here we have a matter on which both christology and pneumatology have a bearing. One of the causes of the direction some recent art has taken as charted, for example, by Peter Fuller, is a breakdown in confidence that the universe is a meaningful enough place for it to be the basis of the creation of beauty.[8] Christology is at the heart of the matter because it is there that the question of the meaning of the material world is raised. Modern pessimism about meaning is based on the very good evidence of sin and evil in the world,[9] but what christology makes possible is a treatment of the question of meaning in the light of the doctrines of the incarnation and the atonement. While the former makes it possible to say that the *material*

---

8. Peter Fuller, *Theoria. Art and the Absence of Grace*, London: Chatto and Windus, 1988. Fuller holds the problem to lie in the breakdown of possibilities for a natural theology as that is expressed in the writing of Ruskin, at its various stages of development. It may be better here to speak of the loss of a theology of nature, for that properly done would involve a christological dimension, as natural theology *simpliciter* would not.

9. It can be argued that much modern pessimism derives by a long and winding process from a doctrine, deriving from Greek philosophy, of the relative unreality of matter. For the evidence, see Colin Gunton, 'Creation and Recreation. An Exploration of some Themes in Aesthetics

world's fundamental meaningfulness is demonstrated
by the fact that the one through whom it took shape
became material, the latter takes with full seriousness
the problem of fallenness and evil. The incarnate dies as
the result of his engagement with a fallen world, and by
his death calls it back to its true destiny. Thus by the
incarnation the material world is affirmed as the place
where there can be meaning, while through the cross of
the crucified it is redeemed from meaninglessness.

The chief basis of human science, technology, craft
and art is therefore christological. The teaching that the
one through whom the world was made became part of
that world, even in its fallenness, affirms the readiness
of that world for human knowledge, action and
shaping. But it must be added that science and art
involve not simply the discovery and shaping of
inherent possibilities, but also the restoration of the
creation to its *telos*, its end which is something over and
above its beginning. Here we return to the question
adumbrated in the discussion of the sacraments, that of
the transformation of matter. As christology is concerned with meaning and redemption, pneumatology
brings us into the realm of transformation. The distinction is not, of course, absolute. Transformation takes
place only as the creation is redeemed from its bondage
to dissolution: the Spirit transforms only in relation to
the work of the crucified. The artist therefore transforms only through a process of burdensome redemption, through wrestling with the recalcitrance of words
and things. Yet because Jesus is raised from the dead
through the action of the Spirit art can properly be
understood as one of the ways by which the Spirit

and Theology', *Modern Theology* 2 (1985), pp. 1–19. A merely natural
theology can concede the case to the opposition by evading the
problems of evil in appealing only to order and beauty.

brings about the *telos* of the creation. (It is no accident that inspiration is not only a religious concept.)

The justification of the distinction that is being made here between the christological and the pneumatological, between the incarnate and saving work of Christ and the transforming action of the Spirit, is that it enables different things to be said. We are enabled by it to speak about both meaning and redemption, both transformation and perfection. As should be clear, the distinction is not a separation, because we are concerned with the action of the one God, and because without mutual illumination neither dimension can be adequately treated. Yet it is a distinction, because the different dimensions of our world, its createdness and teleology, its fallenness and redemption, all require to be given due attention if the ways of human action in the world are to be articulated.

To risk the danger of ending with banal moralism, something must be said in the light of all this about the matter of ecology. The link with the previous discussion is to be found in a common concern to see the end of creation as consisting in its praise of the creator. For theology, therefore, the heart of the ecological question is not to be found in 'saving the planet', which like the rest of the universe is destined to come to an end. Rather, the distinctively Christian contributions to the process are in generating an awareness of the penultimacy of all matters to do with this world of time and space, and yet of the capacity that even this penultimate has to praise the God who made it.

The ecological problem is in large part what it is because we do not do the things that enable the creation to be perfected. Which human actions in the world do and which do not enable this praise is not a question amenable to easy answers. It is easy to give some obvious examples. To turn a desert into a garden is one thing, to turn a rainforest into a desert quite another.

Yet what of our treatment of the animals? May it be right to suggest that the eating of meat is consistent with such an end, but not the rearing of them in factory farms? I use that example not only because it is controversial but also because it raises a central question about human behaviour towards the world. Its unavoidability will be clear if we become aware of the fact, not always noted in the more idealistic discussions of the topic, that ecology will *always* be a problem. All human activity changes the balance of what there is, and should do so, unless we are to see the aim of activity as the achievement of static equilibrium (the apparent aim of Plato's essentially reactionary state and of the prescriptions of some ecologists. Is the loss of any species necessarily and always to be lamented?) There will always be involved in human action both incompatible ends and engagement with the fallenness of all things.

At the heart of this discussion is the matter of destruction. Human activity always involves destruction, not absolutely, of course, for our activity does not violate the law of the conservation of matter, but relatively, in that what we do brings about irreversible changes in the network and dynamics of created reality. The eating of bread and the drinking of wine destroy the food and the drink, just as, indeed, the grain of wheat had first to rot in the ground before the ear of corn could develop for the bread to be made. So it is with all human activity; even conservation, and certainly art, involves the destruction of something. The rightness or otherwise of the eating of meat depends upon whether, and in what way, the killing and eating of animals can, along with other forms of activity that change the structures of the world, be held to be consistent with the praise of God. On the one hand, the eating of meat has nearly always been a feature of human culture, and indeed has been at the centre of the institution of sacrifice, that in which the worship of God essentially consists. On the other hand, it may be argued that the eating of animals, along with their ritual sacrifice, should be abolished because the covenant incorporates them in particularly close ways in human culture. Whatever the conclusion of that argument, there is certainly a strong case for holding that much modern industrialisation of the processes of rearing and killing animals is an offence against the goodness of the creator.

As the inconclusive nature of some of the above arguments will demonstrate, those called to the *dominium terrae* which is the gift of conformity to Christ will not have in their hands a key that will open all doors, a ready reckoner for the solution of all problems. Short of the end, there are no final solutions. The promise is not of solutions, but of the freedom sometimes to share through the Spirit in particular transformations of the world which are signalled by the resurrection of Jesus Christ from the dead. The 'sometimes' is important, because it saves us from the commitment to ultimacy which marks so many of the utterances of modern representatives of the green movement. It is not for us to say where the whole universe or even the whole earth is going. We know in part. There is a 'sometimes' because eschatology is never completely realised, except it be in Christ. And even there, all is in one sense not yet complete. In the second lecture, I pointed out that the logic of the resurrection is that Jesus' story awaits completion. When the parousia will happen and what form it will take is not for us to say. Certainly, it cannot be identified with any of the secular eschatologies of current fashion, whether thermo-nuclear or universal. It may come through one of them, for our theme reminds us that our sacrifice is complete only with our death, as Charles Wesley knew so well. But any treatment of Christ and creation, however fragmentary—as one as brief as this must be—must end with the affirmation that the one through whom the universe came to be, the Word of power by whom it is upheld, is also the one by whom the last word will be said, as he hands over the kingdom to the Father, that God may be all in all.